CREATIVE

BIBLE LESSONS

FROM THE

Old Testament

Other *Creative Bible Lessons* from Youth Specialties

▼▼▼▼▼▼▼▼▼▼▼▼▼▼▼▼▼▼▼▼▼▼▼▼▼▼▼▼▼▼

Creative Bible Lessons on the Life of Christ
Doug Fields

Creative Bible Lessons in John
Janice & Jay Ashcraft

Creative Bible Lessons in Romans
Chap Clark

Other *Creative Bible Lessons* from Youth Specialties

▼▼▼▼▼▼▼▼▼▼▼▼▼▼▼▼▼▼▼▼▼▼▼▼▼▼▼

Creative Bible Lessons on the Life of Christ
Doug Fields

Creative Bible Lessons in John
Janice & Jay Ashcraft

Creative Bible Lessons in Romans
Chap Clark

Creative Bible Lessons in 1 & 2 Corinthians
Marv Penner

Youth Specialties Books, 1224 Greenfield Dr., El Cajon, CA 92021, are published by Zondervan Publishing House, 5300 Patterson Ave. S.E., Grand Rapids, MI 49530.

Library of Congress Cataloging-in-Publication Data

Polich, Laurie.
    Creative Bible lessons from the Old Testament: 12 character studies of surprisingly modern men & women / Laurie Polich.
        p.   cm.
    Includes index.
    ISBN 0-310-22441-1
    1. Bible. O.T.—Biography. 2. Church work with youth. I. Title.
BS571.P65   1998
221.9'2—dc21
[b]
                                                97-32390
                                                  CIP

Edited by J. Cheri McLaughlin
Cover and interior design by Michael Kern

Printed in the United States of America

    00 01 02 03 04 05/ /8 7 6 5

Dedication

To every youth worker I have had the privilege of meeting over the years. You are an inspiration to me.

CONTENTS

Acknowledgments

Special thanks to—

Vivian and Terry McIlraith, who graciously gave me a quiet place to write this book.

Danny Wallen and the Ponderosa summer staff of '97, who supported and encouraged me during the writing of this book.

Genie, Dan, and the Camp Hammer staff, who celebrated with me when I finished writing.

Vicki and Jon Stairs, who continue to be good friends and a great support to my ministry.

Tim McLaughlin and Karla Yaconelli, who faithfully encourage and push to get good resources into youth workers' hands.

The kids in my ministry at First Presbyterian Church, Berkeley, who put up with all my attempts to get them excited about God's Word. I'm happy to say, in looking at your lives now—it worked!

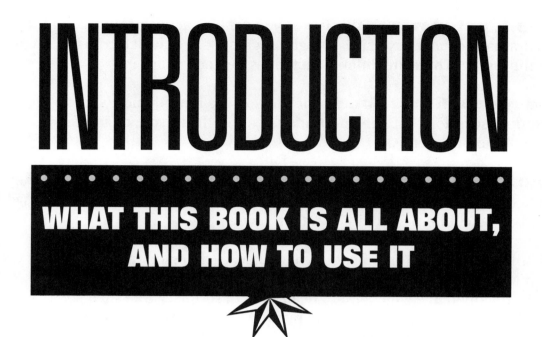

INTRODUCTION

WHAT THIS BOOK IS ALL ABOUT, AND HOW TO USE IT

Chances are if you've picked up this book, you are part of the small but significant segment of the population which spends countless hours figuring out how to make the Bible come alive for a roomful of teenagers. This is a formidable call. The only decision a lot of adults make on Saturday nights is whether to go out to dinner and a movie, or order a pizza and rent a video. You, on the other hand, spend your Saturday nights deciding whether an object lesson or a melodrama fits your Sunday morning lesson best. Or you wrestle with seminary friends over deep theological issues, like how to make Shuffle Your Buns relay tie into a lesson on King Saul.

This book is for people like you, with a passion for God's word and for teenagers. Here are 12 Old Testament lessons that help you communicate the truths of the Bible so that kids not only hear the Word but experience it. I've tried to write sound theology into these lessons, and in such a way as to appeal to a wide range of learning experiences for the kids in your ministry—who all learn in different ways. So with any luck, equipped with 12 complete lesson plans with fresh new ideas at your fingertips, you can get out on a Saturday night every once in a while.

Each lesson in the book follows the same general organization:

• **Intro.** This is the creative hook to get your kids interested in the lesson—such as a game, object lesson, or mixer—with suggestions for making a smooth, logical transition from the intro into your teaching.

• **Bible lesson.** Just about every lesson has an outline for a talk. Although the talk is optional, it contains insight, Scripture references, and ideas for illustrations for however you get across the point of the lesson—whether you give the talk verbatim or deliver it with your own twist. You can even lose the talk altogether and rely on the small-group discussion (see below) to convey the lesson's point.

• **Get up & get moving!** This is a way to get kids actively involved in the lesson through drama, a creative exercise, or a group game—all of which communicate the main point of the lesson. There are different activities for each chapter.

• **Small-group discussion.** In each lesson is a reproducible sheet of questions for small-group discussion. Use the questions as part of the lesson, or as a follow-up discussion for another time.

• **Application.** This is a tool or exercise designed to help kids apply what they've learned to their own lives. There is a different exercise for each lesson, and kids either do it at the end, or take it home and do it on their own.

Within this general organization, of course, each lesson takes a different creative approach to its Old Testament person.

Also included in each chapter are all sorts of scripts, game sheets, and other reproducible materials you can photocopy for use with your youth group. (Just send me a check if you start making money on this stuff.)

So that's it. You know, you're my kind of people—underpaid, overworked, overgrown adolescents crazy enough to prefer the company of teenagers to the adult Sunday school class at your church. I hope you enjoy teaching the rich lessons of the Old Testament as much as I enjoyed putting them together.

SESSION ONE

ABRAHAM
BELIEVE IT OR NOT

Genesis 12:1-7
      15:1-6
      17:1-9

Genesis 21:1-7
      22:1-12

THE LESSON ON
FAITH
HERE'S THE POINT.

Living by faith is not for wimps.

What does it take to live a life of faith? It takes patience when the wait seems endless, hope when things seem impossible, and trust when the circumstances appear insurmountable. Christians are called to a life of ups and downs, of victories and struggles, and ultimately of being a part of something much bigger than our own individual lives. That also describes Abraham's journey—and through his story we can learn what faith is all about.

INTRO
I don't believe it...

You'll need...

- *the video Father of the Bride, Part 2*

You'll need...

- *3 signs as described below*
- *Could it happen? statements on page 12*

Show the humorous video clip from *Father of the Bride, Part 2,* where Steve Martin's and Diane Keaton's characters find out they are going to be middle-aged parents (start tape at 42:35; end tape at 45:27).

Then segue into your game by saying—

When Steve Martin and Diane Keaton find out they're going to be parents, they're surprised because they think they're too old. I'm going to test your expertise in sex education by playing a game.

(The "S" word gets everyone's undivided attention. Trust me, it works every time.)

GAME
Could it happen?

Place these three signs around your room:

Could definitely happen   Could possibly happen   Could never happen

Request students to stand up and move their chairs (if they need to) so they can move freely across the room. Ask them to listen as you read aloud the following seven statements. Tell them they must respond by moving to stand by the sign that expresses their opinion about whether the statement could definitely happen, could possibly happen, or could never happen.

Keep your students listening carefully and responding rapidly by reading quickly through the statements.

1. **It's possible for a 70-year-old man to have a child.**
(Be ready for some kids to reply: "Men don't have children.")

2. **It's possible for a 60-year-old woman to have a child.**

3. **It's possible for a 80-year-old man to have a child with a woman who is 25 years younger than he is.**

4. **It's possible for an 70-year-old woman to have a child with a man who is 15 years younger than she is.**

5. **It's possible for a 90-year-old man to have a child.**

6. **It's possible for a 90-year-old man to have a child with a barren woman.**

7. **It's possible for a 100-year-old man to have a child with a barren woman who is 10 years younger.**

Periodically stop and ask students to explain their responses. (Their answers will let you know what you need to teach in your love, sex, and dating series.) When you get to statement seven, your kids should all be standing by the COULD NEVER HAPPEN sign. Tell them that statement describes Abraham and Sarah when they gave birth to Isaac.

Segue into your Bible lesson by saying—

> **Most of you (with good reason) said there was no chance for that last couple to have a baby. It was hard enough for Steve Martin and Diane Keaton to believe they could have a baby in their 50s! Yet Abraham was 100, Sarah was 90, and they had never been able to have children. But God had promised Abraham that, in spite of his circumstances, he and Sarah would have a son.**
>
> **Why did God wait so long to fulfill his promise? It seems God was as interested in building Abraham's faith as he was in answering his desires. Therefore, God took Abraham through a series of challenges to build him into a great man of faith. He does the same in our lives, too—if we let him.**
>
> **As we look at Abraham's journey, think about your own faith journey...and how much you are able to trust God.**

BIBLE LESSON

Abraham's journey of faith

Although Abraham's story occupies 12 chapters in Genesis, your lesson will focus only on his lessons in faith. If you are giving a talk, here's a suggested outline:

THE MOVE

📓 Genesis 12:1-7 — Describe Abraham's first test of faith and reflect on how it must have felt for him to move after years of living in Ur. (Use an illustration from your own experiences of moving to another town.)

THE PROMISE

📓 Genesis 15:1-6 — Describe the circumstances surrounding God's promise to Abraham.

📓 Genesis 17:1-9 — Explain why (as time passed) it was so difficult for Abraham and Sarah to believe they would actually have a son. (Refer back to the video clip, or add an appropriate personal illustration.)

📓 Genesis 21:1-7 — Ultimately, God honored his promise: Abraham and Sarah did finally have a son.

THE SACRIFICE

📓 Genesis 22:1-12 — Tell the story of when God asked Abraham to sacrifice Isaac.

It seems crazy to us that God would ask Abraham to sacrifice Isaac after all it took to bring him into the world. Yet God wants us to hold things loosely, always putting him first. (Talk about how hard it is to do that with some things).

Abraham knew he could trust God because of all the things he had seen God do. Even when we don't understand what God is doing, God calls us to trust and obey. In the long run, we'll often understand why.

SMALL-GROUP DISCUSSION

Abraham's journey of faith

You'll need...

- *copies of Abraham's Journey of Faith—Small Group Q's 1.1*
- *pencils*
- *extra Bibles*

In the real world, there's seldom time for both a complete talk and a full-blown small-group discussion. Let your small-group facilitators pick and choose from among the **Small-Group Q's**, or save the discussion for another time.

GET UP & GET MOVING!

Help your kids experience the lesson of faith and trust by using one of the options explained below. Option 1 can be done right in the youth room. Option 2 requires a climbing wall and equipment.

Option 1: Backward leaps of faith

Set the chair and table facing the group. Choose a fairly small student to come to the front. Blindfold the volunteer. Stand six to

You'll need...

- *1 folding chair*
- *a table*
- *at least 8 people (recruit adults for smaller groups)*

eight kids as close together as possible in two parallel lines in front of the volunteer. Gripping each other's forearms, the group members form a sturdy platform.

Face the volunteer away from the group and ask him to fall backwards onto the arms of the group. Instruct the group to catch the student. Next, help the student onto the chair that's facing the group. Once more ask the student to turn his back to the group and fall onto their arms. Finally, help the student onto the table. In the same way the student turns around and falls back onto the group one last time. (Make sure this begins and ends as an object lesson, not a lawsuit.)

Debrief your group by asking these questions:

- What did you observe about what we just did?

- What (if anything) does this exercise illustrate about faith? (By staging three increasingly more risky falls, the volunteer learns by experience to trust the group. The parallel, of course, is that God builds our faith by taking us through bigger and bigger challenges as we learn to trust him more and more.)

Option 2: Rock climbing

You'll need...

- *a beginner's rock-climbing site (5.5 and 5.6 routes are good for this lesson) or an indoor climbing gym*

- *climbing equipment—harnesses, ropes, shoes, helmets (in climbing gyms, available to rent)*

- *a certified or highly experienced instructor or coach*

For a concrete experience of what faith is all about, take students rock climbing outdoors or at a gym. Climbing while they're on belay (that is, harnessed to a rope with an anchored partner at the other end) or rappelling (lowering oneself backward off a rock) is a lesson in trust. The only way they learn to trust the rope, the belayer, and themselves is by resting their weight on the harness.

It's the same with trusting God—you won't know whether you can really trust him until you take a step of faith. Rock climbing can anchor that truth in a student's mind for a long time. (For information on group rock climbing, call Christian Wilderness Adventures at 800-884-8483.)

APPLICATION
Faith detector

You'll need...

- *copies of Faith Detector—Making Connections 1.2*

Pass out copies of the **Faith Detector** on which students can graph their faith journey over the next week. Ask them to bring their worksheet back to youth group next week and share with their small group what their graph looks like. (Optional: For kids who would like to track their spiritual growth over a longer time, provide additional copies of the chart.)

ABRAHAM'S JOURNEY OF FAITH

Read aloud or skim the following Scriptures.
Use what you learn to discuss the related questions.

Genesis 12:2,3

1   The first time God speaks to Abraham, he tells him to move (v.1) and then gives him a list of promises. List the promises God makes to Abraham if he chooses to obey God.

2   Look at the kinds of moves listed below. Rate them from least difficult to most difficult.

——— Moving to a different school
——— Moving to a different room in your house
——— Moving to a different country
——— Moving to a different grade
——— Moving to a different neighborhood
——— Moving to a different state
——— Moving to a different group of friends

3   Which of these moves have you experienced?

4   Which did Abraham experience?

5   How do you think Abraham's move affected his relationship with God?

Genesis 15:1-6

6   What was Abraham's second test of faith?

7   Why was this promise hard to believe?

Genesis 15:6

8   According to this verse, is it our actions or our belief that makes us righteous before God?

9   How do we become righteous?

Skim Genesis 16

10   What did Abraham and Sarah do to try to help God fulfill his promise?

11   Do you think their intentions were good or bad?

12   List the positive and negative results of their actions.

Genesis 21:1-7

13   Why do you think God waited so long to fulfill his promise?

14   How do you think the delay affected Abraham's and Sarah's faith?

Genesis 22:1,2

15   After all that Abraham had been through, how do you think he was feeling when he heard what God said?

Genesis 22:3-8

16   Despite what Abraham was feeling, he obeyed God. Why do you think he did?

Genesis 22:10-12

17   How did God respond to Abraham when he saw his obedience?

18   After looking at Abraham's faith journey, think about where you are in your faith. On a scale of 1 to 10 (1 being no faith and 10 being a lot of faith), where would you put yourself?

1   2   3   4   5   6   7   8   9   10

19   What would help you increase your faith?

Faith Detector

A lot of faith

10
9
8
7
6
5
4
3
2
1

A little faith

| SUN | MON | TUE | WED | THUR | FRI | SAT |

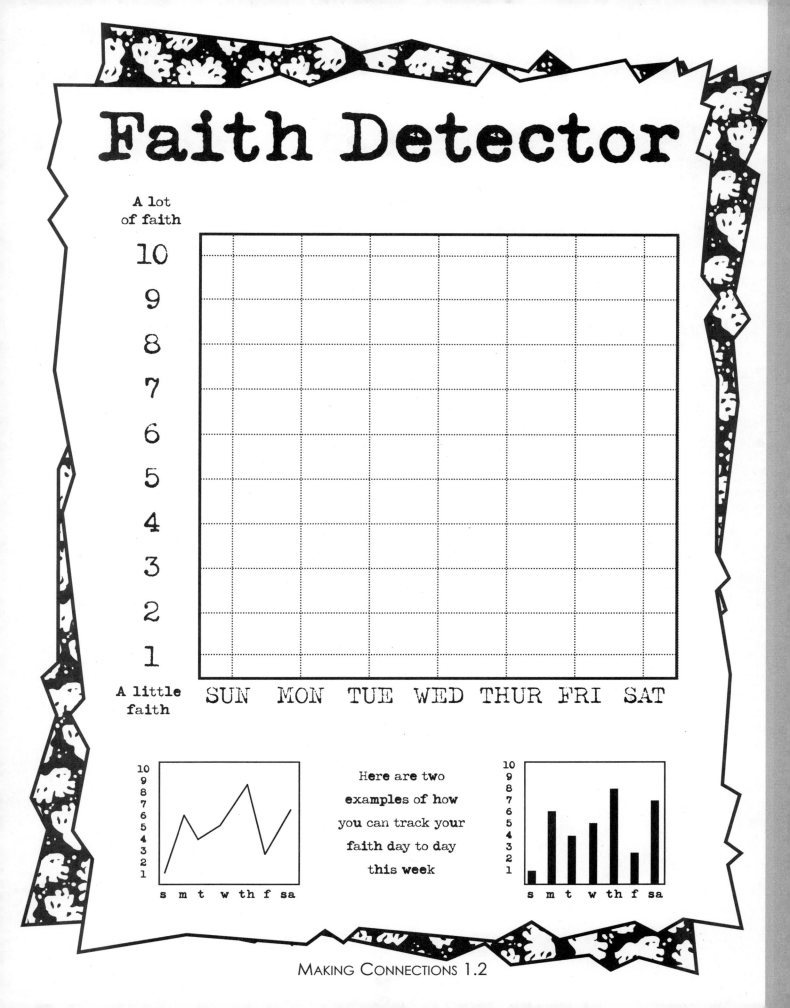

Here are two examples of how you can track your faith day to day this week

SESSION TWO

JACOB
IN THE DRIVER'S SEAT

Genesis 25:19-34
27:1-35

Genesis 29:14-30
32:22-32

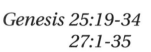

Control the ring

Get your students to arrange their chairs into a circle. (Or into several circles if you have a large group. You'll need at least 6-8 kids in a circle to make this work, plus one finger ring and one string length per circle of kids.) One student—"it"—stands in the middle of the circle. Now unwind a length of string that everyone around the circle holds. Thread a large ring onto the string, then tie the string's ends together, creating a loop. The ring needs to slide easily along the string. Everyone around the circle grabs hold of the string with both hands.

You'll need...

For each circle of students:
- *A large finger ring*
- *A long piece of string*

Now the game starts. The circle members slide the ring along the string, passing it to each other under their hands, subtly, so that poor "it" in the middle can't make out whose hands the ring is under. If "it" wants to make a guess where the ring is, she walks to the circle and taps the hand she thinks is covering the ring. If she's right, she trades places with the hapless circle sitter.

Once a group gets the hang of it, they can stay pretty much in control of the ring—and the game. Meanwhile, out in the middle of the circle by himself, "it" will probably feel pretty much out of control. In fact, unless your "it" is particularly shrewd or your group particularly bumbling, you may have to call time yourself and simply announce a new "it" every few minutes.

HERE'S THE POINT.

We all wrestle with the issue of control now and then.

Whether it's something we want to have, something we want to happen, or something we're waiting for, we often try to get ahead of God by taking into our own hands the control of our lives. And sometimes it looks like it works.

Jacob took a shot at making his life turn out the way he thought it should, but he discovered that winning at life means letting God lead. God is ultimately in control of our lives—whether we act like it or not. His plan unfolds in his way. Perhaps we can learn from Jacob's lesson by reflecting on his story—and avoid hip-replacement surgery (check out Genesis 32:25).

Segue into your Bible lesson by saying—

Those of you who were "it" may have felt pretty helpless—probably because you weren't in control. And, of course, it was easy to feel in control when you were part of the circle.

Now just how much control of your own life do you demand? Take Jacob, for instance—he actually *wrestled* God over the issue of control. As we look at Jacob's story, recall the times you've wrestled God for control in your life—and how you can learn from Jacob what it means to truly win.

BIBLE LESSON

And in this corner...

Although Jacob's story occupies 10 chapters in Genesis, your lesson focuses only on his struggle for control. If you are giving a talk, here's a suggested outline.

JACOB'S BIRTH

📖 Genesis 25:19-34

🕴 The circumstances surrounding Jacob's birth suggest that Jacob's struggle was a control thing (a clue that much of our personality is with us when we are born, as the writer of Psalm 139 reveals).

📖 Genesis 27:1-35

🕴 God previewed Jacob's future when he told Rebekah that her older twin would be a servant of the younger twin. However, even though Jacob's claim on the birthright was secure with God, Jacob fought to get it as soon as he had the chance. (Give a personal illustration of getting ahead of God—one that clearly shows how difficult it is to "let go and let God.")
Just as Jacob tricked Esau, Laban tricked Jacob.

JACOB'S MARRIAGE

📖 Genesis 29:14-30

🕴 Not only did Laban give the wrong sister in marriage to Jacob, but Laban required Jacob to work for him another seven years to earn Rachel.

🕴 Maybe God is cautioning us that what goes around, comes around.

JACOB'S WRESTLING MATCH

i Genesis 32:22-32

By the time Jacob literally wrestled with God, he'd already done a lot of wrestling in his life. In this passage, Jacob is renamed Israel— "one who has power with God." Jacob struggled with God and overcame, but not without injury.

Perhaps God preserved Jacob's story partly to counsel Christians that, in the end, accepting our weakness is actually our strength.

SMALL-GROUP DISCUSSION

Jacob's wrestling match

You'll need...

- copies of **Jacob's Wrestling Match— Small Group Q's 2.1**
- pencils
- extra Bibles

In the real world, there's seldom time for both a complete talk and a full-blown small group discussion. Let your small group facilitators pick and choose from among the **Small Group Q's,** or save the discussion for another time.

If you do the discussion, keep the flow of the meeting going by setting up the obstacle course for the **Get Up & Get Moving!** activity while students are in their small groups.

GET UP & GET MOVING!

Blind walk

Using chairs, tables, and random objects, set up a mini obstacle course in your youth room or outside. Make sure a clear path goes from the beginning of the course to the end.

You'll need...

- a few chairs and tables
- other objects to form an obstacle course

Break the group into two teams. Blindfold the members of the first team, then ask members of the second team to be the guide for one of the blindfolded students. As the pairs enter the obstacle course, the blindfolded students walk behind their guides, placing their hands on the guide's shoulders. The guides lead each blindfolded student through the obstacle course.

Then turn the tables by blindfolding the other member of the pair instead. This time, when the students walk the obstacle course, the guides follow behind the blindfolded students, telling them where to go—no touching. Theoretically (meaning that you can't predict whether a youth worker's brainstorm will actually work on any given night), the second group will have a much tougher time making it through the course.

Debrief your group by saying—

> **If you had to go through the obstacle course one more time, which way would you rather do it—with your guide in front or in back? Why?**
>
> **Of course it's easier with your guide in front. Yet, even having experienced that reality physically, we struggle to speed past God's leadership. Like Jacob, though, the obstacles we encounter teach us that, in the long run, the best way to live is to let God lead us. The choice is ours.**

APPLICATION

The tandem bike

Read aloud from **The Tandem Bike.** Then read the following question and possible responses.

You'll need...

- *copies of The Tandem Bike— Making Connections 2.2*

■ ■ ■ ■ ■ ■ ■

If you and God were on a tandem bike riding through life, where would you be?
- **I'm in the back with God in front.**
- **I'm in front, with God in the back.**
- **We keep switching places depending on the condition of the road.**
- **I'm in front, and I'm not sure where God is.**

JACOB'S WRESTLING MATCH

**Read aloud or skim the following Scriptures.
Use what you learn to discuss the related questions.**

Genesis 25:21-23

1 How did Jacob come into the world?

2 What does his arrival tell you about Jacob's personality?

Genesis 25:29-34

3 As God's prophecy for Jacob (Genesis 25:23) began to come true, was it more of Jacob's doing or God's doing?

4 How do you think God felt about what Jacob did?

Genesis 27:1-35

5 Assign five students to read aloud the parts of Isaac, Esau, Jacob, Rebekah, and the narrator.

6 On a scale of one to five, rate the following people—1 for the person you believe to be *most* responsible for what happened with Jacob, and 5 for the person you believe to be *least* responsible for what happened.

—————————— Rebekah
—————————— Isaac
—————————— Jacob
—————————— Esau
—————————— God

7 Discuss with your group why you rated them the way you did.

Genesis 28:10-17

8 Do you think Jacob's dream had an impact on his relationship with God? Why/Why not?

Genesis 29:16-30

9 Take turns reading aloud the story about what Jacob went through to get the woman he loved.

10 In the space below, write out the obstacles Jacob had to overcome to marry Rachel.

Obstacle #1 _____
Obstacle #2 _____
Obstacle #3 _____

11 Why do you think Jacob ran into obstacles?

12 What do you think God was trying to teach Jacob?

Genesis 32:9-12

13 Leaving Laban and going home meant that Jacob would see his brother Esau again. Read how Jacob prayed when he and his two wives paused on their journey to Jacob's home.

Genesis 32:22-30

14 Read aloud the passage and discuss why God answered Jacob by wrestling with him.

15 What happened to Jacob during the wrestling match?

16 Part of the human condition is our urge to control our own lives. Invite each student in the group to share one thing in their life they have trouble giving over to God's control.

THE TANDEM BIKE

At first, I saw God as my observer, my judge,
Keeping track of the things I did wrong,
So as to know whether I merited heaven or hell when I die.
He was out there sort of like a president.
I recognized his picture when I saw it, but I really didn't know him.

But later on when I met Christ,
It seemed as though life was rather like a bike ride,
A tandem bike,
And I noticed that Christ was in the back helping me pedal.

I don't know when it was that he suggested we change places,
But life has not been the same since.
When I had control, I knew the way.
It was rather boring, but predictable,
The shortest distance between two points.
But when he took the lead, he knew delightful long cuts—
Up mountains, and through rocky places at breakneck speeds.
It was all I could do to hang on!
Even though it looked like madness, he said "Pedal."
I worried and asked, "Where are you taking me?"
He laughed and didn't answer, and I started to learn to trust.
I forgot my boring life and entered into the adventure.
And when I'd say, "I'm scared," he'd lean back and touch my hand.
He took me to people with gifts that I needed,
Gifts of healing, acceptance, and joy.
They gave me gifts to take on my journey,
And we were off again.
He'd say, "Give the gifts away; they're extra baggage, too much weight."
So I did, to the people we met,
And I found that in giving I received—but still our burden was light.

I did not trust him, at first, in control of my life. I thought he'd wreck it.
But he knows biking secrets, knows how to take sharp corners,
Knows how to jump to clear rocks,
Even knows how to fly to shorten scary passages.
And I am learning to shut up and pedal in the strangest places.
And I'm beginning to enjoy the view—and the cool breeze on my face—
With my companion Jesus Christ.
And when I'm sure I just can't do any more, he just smiles and says,
"Pedal."

—Author unknown

SESSION THREE

JOSEPH
THE WAITING GAME

Genesis chapter 37   Genesis 41:1-40
          chapter 39   42:1-8
          chapter 40   45:1-5

INTRO

It's gotta hurt

Post the following pictures on the wall or bulletin board where students can see them when they walk in:

You'll need...

- *four pictures listed at right*
- *scrap paper*
- *pens*
- *a can*
- *small prizes*

- **a muscular body (a man would probably be the best choice)**
- **a newborn baby**
- **a high school diploma**
- **an Olympic medal**

Place the scrap paper, pens, and can near the pictures. Post the following instructions near the pictures:

What do these things have in common?
If you think you know—
1. Write your guess on a piece of paper.
2. Sign your name.
3. Fold it.
4. Put the paper in the can.
**   If we draw your guess and it's right, you'll get a prize.**

One by one, draw the guesses out of the can until you find one that is correct.

THE LESSON ON
PERSEVERANCE

HERE'S THE POINT

Trials and temptations are meant to make us strong.

Staying power is what separates those who make it through life successfully from those who buckle under pressure. Helping you hang in there when the going gets rough is God's way of giving your spirit a workout.
     Joseph's life is an example of what it means to persevere under pressure and come out on top.

Reward the student who wrote the correct answer (food is a perennially favorite reward—Smarties, M&Ms, a donut).

The answer should go something like this: **Each picture represents a reward that came with perseverance and pain.**

Segue into your Bible lesson by saying—

> **When you hear "No pain, no gain" or "Go for the burn," what do you think of? Athletic prowess? Buns of steel? Staying in top physical condition?**
>
> **How about staying in good spiritual condition? Spirit workouts mimic body workouts—good results come only with perseverance, struggle, and yes, even some pain.**
>
> **Long before muscle magazines, Joseph knew this truth. Though one trial after another confronted Joseph, he remained faithful every step of the way. In the end, Joseph received the blessings he longed for. His story models how to persevere under pressure—no matter how difficult your circumstances get.**

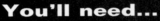

BIBLE LESSON & GET UP & GET MOVING!

The story of Joe and his bros

You'll need...

- *copies of the script "The Story of Joe and His Bros"—Script 3.1*
- *stools or chairs*
- *10 to 13 readers*

Done in reader's theater style, this humorous version of Joseph's life in four scenes actually stays pretty true to the text. Place stools (or chairs) in the front of the room. Recruit your cast members on the spot to sit up front and bring the story to life.

SMALL-GROUP DISCUSSION

Perseverance under pressure

You'll need...

- copies of **Joseph: Perseverance under Pressure— Small Group Q's 3.2**
- pencils
- extra Bibles

How close are the students in your group? Some of the questions in **Joseph: Perseverance under Pressure** could lead to a deep level of personal sharing if the students feel they can trust their group. Think through the questions and decide ahead of time which ones your students are most likely to respond to candidly.

APPLICATION

Fight or flight?

Is the best response to temptation *fight* or *flight?*

    In small groups (or with everyone if your group is small), discuss or debate the best thing to do if faced with any of the following situations. Should a person flee the situation or stay and be strong in the midst of it?

- *(for girls)* **You're at your boyfriend's house because his parents are gone for the weekend, and he wants you to have sex tonight.**

- *(for guys)* **You're all alone with your best friend's girl friend (to whom you've always been attracted), and she wants you to kiss her.**

- **You're at a party where you're the only one who's not drinking.**

- **Your non-Christian friends (who like to party) are going away for the weekend to ski, and they want you to come.**

- **You're sitting in class taking a test, surrounded by friends who are all cheating. Then your teacher leaves the room.**

- *(for girls)* **You're staying at a friend's house, and she lies to her parents so the two of you can go to an unchaperoned party.**

- *(for guys)* **You're staying at a friend's house, and he pulls out a stack of Penthouse magazines.**

THE STORY OF JOE AND HIS BROS

CAST

Narrator, your best reader—guy or girl

Joe, a guy who can ham it up

Joe's Bros, 2-5 guys who can read together

Papa Jake, small part for any guy

Pot's wife, a girl who can ham it up

Cup gal, a girl—should read pretty well

Baker boy, a guy—should read pretty well

Pharaoh, a girl or guy—small part

Sign carrier, no lines—fun part

PROPS

Four signs, each with the title of one of the four scenes in the reader's theater

SCENE 1: (NOT SO) SWEET DREAMS

SCENE 2: (NOT SO) SAFE SEX

SCENE 3: (NOT SO) HAPPY TIMES

SCENE 4: (NOT SO) BAD AFTER ALL

Scene 1: (Not So) Sweet Dreams
Genesis 37

NARRATOR: *(invites audience to hum along as he or she sings to the tune of "The Beverly Hillbillies")*
Now this is the story of a man named Joe
Who was sold as a slave for telling dreams to his bros.
And just when he thought he'd had enough strife
Out from the bed popped Potiphar's wife.
> Sex, that is
> Boss's wife
> Big no-no
As she grabbed his clothes, he decided he'd bail,
And sadly enough ended up in jail.
But it doesn't end there—we can all take heart.
And if I stop this silly rhyme, the show can finally start.

Sign carrier walks across stage with a sign that says,
SCENE 1: (NOT SO) SWEET DREAMS

JOE:	Hey boys! It's me again—back with another dream.
JOE'S BROS:	*(sarcastically, in unison)* We can hardly wait.
JOE:	Well, first we were binding sheaves, and your sheaves bowed to my sheaf.
JOE'S BROS:	*(angrily)* What a bunch of sheaves!
JOE:	*(getting more excited)* Then your stars bowed to my stars!
CAST:	*(all together)* Star light, star bright!
JOE:	*(loudly, arms outstretched)* My star is shining bright.
CAST:	Star light, star bright!
JOE'S BROS:	*(roll their eyes and say to each other)* He's outta here tonight!
PAPA JAKE:	*(turns to Joe's Bros)* What'd you say, boys?
JOE'S BROS:	*(nervously)* Uh…we said, "Our Joe is outta sight!"
PAPA JAKE:	He sure is. That's my boy!
NARRATOR:	Unfortunately for Papa Jake, he was a little hard of hearing and more than a little in denial of his obvious favoritism. So Joe's bros sold Joe to the Ishmaelites, who ate the deal up like a bunch of Termites. And they sold him to a man named Potiphar, which brings us to Scene 2—and Joe's encounter with Potiphar's wife.

Scene 2: (Not So) Safe Sex
Genesis 39

Sign carrier walks across stage with a sign that says,
SCENE 2: (NOT SO) SAFE SEX

POT'S WIFE:	Come here, handsome, and lie with me.	
JOE:	Sorry, ma'am. I never tell a lie.	
POT'S WIFE:	That's not the kind of lying I'm talking about…	*page 2*

JOE:	*(catching on)* Oh! Well, I don't do that, either. Especially not with the boss's wife.
POT'S WIFE:	How about if I pressure you day after day?
JOE:	Listen, Potiphar's wife—hey, don't you have a name?
POT'S WIFE:	*(dramatically, trying to evoke sympathy)* I do, but I'm not important enough for anyone to know it. I'm just known as Potiphar's wife.
JOE:	*(sarcastically)* Poor baby!
POT'S WIFE:	No baby. I practice safe sex. So what do you say, big boy? How about one for the road?
JOE:	The road? Yes. The bed? No!
NARRATOR:	At this point, Potiphar's wife got desperate and began quoting old love songs.
POT'S WIFE:	*(sadly)* If you leave me now, you'll take away the very heart of me.
JOE:	And if I stay, I'll lose a lot more than that!
POT'S WIFE:	You'll be sorry.
JOE:	*(loudly, with conviction)* Maybe, but at least <u>my</u> name will be in the Bible.
NARRATOR:	Then Joe ran out of the house, leaving his cloak in the hands of a sexually frustrated woman whose name we'll never know. But alas—by doing the right thing, Joe ended up in the wrong place. Which takes us to Scene 3.

Scene 3: (Not So) Happy Times
Genesis 40

Sign carrier walks across stage with a sign that says,
SCENE 3: (NOT SO) HAPPY TIMES

JOE:	*(dramatically)* Woe is me. I've been beaten, sold, seduced, and thrown in jail. *(then happily)* Oh well. Might as well make the best of it.

page 3

NARRATOR:	And so Joe decided that, if he was going to be a prisoner, he'd be the best prisoner there ever was.
JOE:	*(with determination)* I'll be the best prisoner there ever was!
NARRATOR:	But soon he was joined by Cup Gal and Baker Boy.
CUP GAL:	*(steps forward out of line, with enthusiasm)* I'm the Cup Gal!
BAKER BOY:	*(steps up next to her)* And I'm the fabulous Baker Boy!
NARRATOR:	After introducing themselves, they told Joseph about their troubling dreams.
CUP GAL & BAKER BOY:	We had some troubling dreams!
JOE:	Do tell!
CUP GAL:	I'll go first. *(slowly, with dramatic emphasis)* My dream was about vines and grapes and Pharaoh's cup. Then Pharaoh came and drank it up.
BAKER BOY:	Does that mean I have to make my dream rhyme, too?
JOE:	Wait your turn, Baker Boy. *(turns to Cup Gal)* Good news, Cup Gal. You'll be back on top very soon! *(gives her a high five)*
BAKER BOY:	I'm next, Joe. *(dramatically)* My dream was about bread and birds and Pharaoh's basket, but Pharaoh didn't come—
JOE:	—'cause he was making a casket.
BAKER BOY:	*(sadly)* Uh-oh. Bad news, right?
JOE:	*(puts his arm around Baker Boy, sympathetically)* Sorry, Baker Boy. But you <u>were</u> fabulous for a couple of paragraphs in Genesis chapter 40. Definitely added to the story line.
BAKER BOY:	*(cheers up some)* Thanks.
JOE:	And Cup Gal—don't forget me when you're back in the

SCRIPT 3.1

	palace.
CUP GAL:	I will for a couple years, but eventually I'll come out of my selfish stupor to think of you again. Bye-bye!
NARRATOR:	And so for two full years, Joe stayed the best prisoner there ever was.
JOE:	*(dramatically, with feeling)* I was the best prisoner there ever was!
NARRATOR:	But then Pharaoh had a dream. Which takes us to our final act.

Scene 4: (Not So) Bad after All
Genesis 41:1-40; 42:1-8; 45:1-5

Sign carrier walks across stage with a sign that says,
SCENE 4: (NOT SO) BAD AFTER ALL

PHARAOH:	*(loudly, in the style of Martin Luther King Jr.)* I had a dream…
CUP GAL:	Oh—that reminds me of Joe!
PHARAOH:	But I haven't told it to you yet.
CUP GAL:	Well, don't tell it to me—tell it to Joe!
NARRATOR:	Unfortunately for Joe, he was still stuck in Scene 3.
PHARAOH:	Who's Joe?
JOE:	*(dreamily)* I was the best prisoner there ever was…
NARRATOR:	So Pharaoh went over to Joe and slapped him out of it.
PHARAOH:	Wake up, boy. I had a dream: there were fat cows, skinny cows, and grains bunched in sevens.
JOE:	To interpret this dream, I'll look to the heavens. *(looks up)* God, you're on!

page 5

SCRIPT 3.1

NARRATOR:	And so it came to pass that Joe interpreted the dream with God's help—and consequently became head of Pharaoh's palace. And then one day Joe's brothers showed up there in Egypt. But they had no idea who he was. They just came 'cause they were hungry.
JOE'S BROS:	*(making doorbell sound)* Ding dong!
JOE:	Greeting, boys!
JOE'S BROS:	*(they drop to their knees desperately in front of Joe)* Please, sir—can you spare some food?
JOE:	*(to audience)* They have no idea who I am!
JOE'S BROS:	*(to each other)* We have no idea who he is!
NARRATOR:	Joe had every right to let them starve. But he thought over his life and realized that through all the bad, God intended it for good. So he made himself known to them and said:
JOE:	It's me, guys! You know, the sheaves, the stars—remember that crazy dream?
JOE'S BROS:	*(look at each other nervously)* Uh-oh.
JOE:	Don't be afraid. I won't treat you the way you treated me. And because of that, <u>my</u> story will take up 10 chapters in Genesis, while <u>your</u> story will be squeezed into two. So let's have a group hug and sing "We Are One in the Bond of Love"! *(all hug)*
NARRATOR:	And so it came to pass that the drama was finally over. But the real story lives on and on. Let's give a big hand to our players…and an even bigger hand to God!

End

JOSEPH: PERSEVERANCE UNDER PRESSURE

Read aloud or skim the following Scriptures.
Use what you learn to discuss the related questions.

Genesis 37:1-11

1   Do you think Joseph's brothers were justified in their anger? Why/Why not?

Genesis 37:12-36

2   Joseph's brothers sold him into slavery because they were jealous. Have you ever been jealous of someone else? If so, how did you handle it?

3   Is it possible to keep from getting jealous of others? If so, how?

Genesis 39:2

4   The Lord was with Joseph, even though he had been abandoned by his brothers and sold as a slave. What does that tell you about God's presence in our lives?

Genesis 39:6-18

5   After reading aloud the story of Joseph and Potiphar's wife, make a list of all the things we can learn about temptation from this story.

6   Have you ever felt pressured to give in to a temptation? If so, did the pressure come from yourself, your circumstances, your relationships, or your friends?

7   How did you handle the pressure to do wrong?

8   What help (if any) does Joseph's story give for how you could handle pressure to do wrong in the future?

9   Joseph ended up being punished for doing the right thing. Has that ever happened to you or anyone you know?

10   If you had a choice of doing the right thing and getting punished, or doing the wrong thing and getting rewarded, what do you think you would do? (Try to be honest). What do you hope you would do?

Genesis 45:1-5

11   In the end, Joseph was rewarded for his perseverance with a powerful position through which he could help many people. Even though he could have taken revenge on his brothers, he forgave them. Why did he do that?

12   What would you have done if you were Joseph?

And finally...

13   Do you think it's easier to pay someone back for what they did or to forgive them? Why?

14   Does forgiveness or revenge show more strength?

15   Do you feel better after paying back someone who really deserved it or after forgiving that person? (Ask everyone in the group to share their opinion.)

16   What one thing did you learn from Joseph's life that you can apply to your own life? How will you apply it?

SESSION FOUR

MOSES
BENCHWARMER TO FIRST STRING

Exodus chapters 3-14

Moses burned __what__?

Without even hinting to your students at the content of the Mad Lib, read

You'll need...

- *a copy of the Mad Lib: Moses and the Burning Bush— Making Connections 4.1*
- *a pencil*
- *a Bible*

aloud only the small-print descriptions on the Mad Lib, and fill in the blanks above each description with words or phrases your students suggest. Then thank them for contributing to a retelling, in their own words, of the story of Moses and the burning bush. But before you read the undoubtedly bizarre result, say that you're going to first read Exodus 3:1-12 to let them see how close their retelling comes to the real story. Then read the Mad Lib version. Not only is this a sneaky way to get them to listen carefully to the Bible, but it's good for a few laughs as well.

Segue into your lesson by saying—

This story is almost as crazy as a Mad Lib when you read it the way it is! But amazingly, it's true—that's exactly how God called Moses. But Moses had trouble believing he was the best person for the job. He was insecure in his leadership ability, uncertain about his strength, and self-conscious about the way he spoke. How could God use a stuttering shepherd to accomplish such a great task?

TRUST

HERE'S THE POINT ▲

Often God uses the least likely person to do great things.

Moses might have been voted least likely to make a great contribution to his people, Israel. After all, having been raised in all the opulence of Pharaoh's palace, he was used to the easy life. Nevertheless, God chose Moses to bring his people out of Egypt. He wasn't looking for someone who could do it on his own; rather, God was looking for someone who would have to trust him.

You could say that Moses was most qualified to lead because he was least qualified. That leaves the focus where it should be—on God. Moses' trust in God made the reluctant stammerer into one of the greatest leaders in Jewish history.

In what way are you like Moses? How have your insecurities stopped you from going ahead with something God wanted you to do? Through Moses' story, God assures us that our weaknesses, instead of being a liability, can be the way God displays his power! All we need to do is trust him.

When Moses learned to simply say yes to God—just as he was—God made him one of the most powerful leaders in history.

BIBLE LESSON

Inadequate but called

Although Moses' life story takes up the entire book of Exodus, your lesson will focus only on how Moses came to obey God's call (despite Moses' reservations), and on how God displayed his power through Moses' weakness. Here's a possible outline for teaching the story of Moses:

THE CALL

📖 Exodus chapters 3 and 4

🚶 Talk through a few of the excuses Moses made when God asked him to lead Israel out of Egypt (didn't feel qualified, didn't think Pharaoh would believe him, felt insecure about the way he spoke).

🚶 Tell about a time when you felt scared or insecure about something God called you to do.

🚶 Talk about some of the least likely people God has called to do great things (Billy Graham, Mother Teresa, Chuck Colson).

THE PLAGUES

📖 Exodus chapters 7-12

🚶 Talk about the different ways God showed his power to Pharaoh and the Egyptians. Emphasize that God took care of convincing Pharaoh, just as he promised Moses he would. All Moses had to do was trust God.

🚶 Describe the first celebration of the Passover (Exodus 12) and explain that Jews celebrate that occasion to this day.

🚶 Explain that the Passover lamb, whose blood the Jews painted on their doorposts as a protection from death (Exodus 12:21-23), was symbolic of Jesus' blood, which saves us from spiritual death.

CUE TIP

Illustrate your **Bible Lesson** with a clip from *The Ten Commandments*, starring Charlton Heston as Moses. The parting of the Red Sea is an especially dramatic scene. To extend your lesson, show the whole video at an overnighter.

THE DELIVERANCE

 Exodus chapter 14

The parting of the Red Sea was a dramatic climax to Moses' call, showing how Moses then trusted the power of the Lord and how the Lord displayed his power in spite of soldiers and the Sea.

Moses then became clear about who was really in charge—and from there on out (with only a couple lapses), he depended entirely on the Lord.

GET UP & GET MOVING!

Tasks and handicaps

You'll need...

- *copies of Tasks and Handicaps— Making Connections 4.2*
- *bubble gum*
- *soda crackers*
- *twine or thin rope*
- *a blindfold*
- *20 pencils and a sheet of paper*
- *a bowl of cereal with milk*

Cut out the squares on the worksheet. Each square has instructions paired with a handicap. Put the squares in a box, then ask each of your students draw one out. Tell them not to show anyone their squares. Tell students to each try to complete their task with the handicap they've been given. If you have more students than squares, make additional copies and have more than one student do each task. (Be sure you have enough props.) The student who completes her task first (with her handicap) is the winner.

Segue into your **Small-Group Discussion** by saying—

During this exercise, all of you experienced what it was like to do something you felt inadequate to do. Moses experienced that, too. When God called him to lead the people out of Egypt, he had to overcome his slowness of speech and lack of eloquence to do so. By overcoming these obstacles, Moses learned to trust God. As you discuss the following questions, think about the obstacles you need to overcome in order to trust God.

Overcoming obstacles & learning to trust

You'll need...

- *copies of* **Moses: Overcoming Obstacles and Learning to Trust—Small Group Q's 4.3**

- *pencils*

- *extra Bibles*

Running short on time?
- Use only a few of the worksheet questions
- Or spend time developing the more personal **Application,** saving the discussion for another time

Moses, next time wash your feet first.

APPLICATION

What gets in the way?

Invite the group to call out different obstacles to faith that a person might run into—fears, insecurities, relationships, temptations, other emotions or experiences that stop them from being the person God wants them to be. Then allow five minutes or so of silence (or play a meditative CD) for students to write on their papers the obstacles that hinder them *personally* from trusting God. Ask them to fold their list into their Bible or their school notebook. Their assignment this week is to regularly review the list and pray for God's help to overcome their obstacles.

You'll need...

- *half-sheets of paper*

- *pencils*

Moses and the Burning Bush
M A D   L I B

This is the story of Moses, a _____ , who felt he was too _____
(a profession of some kind)   (adjective)
to be used by God. One day God spoke to Moses from a burning _____ ,
(noun)
He said, "_____! Come over here and take off your _____ .You
(proper name)   (article of clothing)
are standing on holy _____ ." Moses knew God was speaking to him
(noun)
because he was the only _____ who was there.
(noun)

So Moses _____ over to the bush and hid his _____
(action verb in past tense)   (body part)
because he was afraid to look at God. The Lord said, "I have seen the
_____ of my people in Egypt, and have heard them _____ -ing because
(plural noun)   (verb)
of their suffering. So I have come to rescue them from the _____
(group of people from
_____ and bring them out of that land into a _____ and _____
another country)   (adjective)   (adjective)
land flowing with _____ and _____ ."
(beverage)   (food)

"So now, _____ ! I am sending you to _____ to bring
(one word command)   (a foreign country)
my _____ out of Egypt."
(plural noun)

But Moses said, "Who am I that I should _____ and bring your
(action verb)
_____ out of Egypt?"
(same plural noun as before)

And God said, "I will be with _____ . And this will be your sign:
(proper noun)
When you have _____ the people out of Egypt, you will worship
(verb in past tense)
_____ on this mountain. Then you will know it is I who sent you."
(name of someone you respect)

TASKS AND HANDICAPS

TASK: Run around the room 2 times. **HANDICAP:** Your feet must be tied together.	**TASK:** Sing the national anthem through 3 times. **HANDICAP:** You must be chewing 6 pieces of bubble gum.	**TASK:** Eat an entire bowl of cereal with milk. **HANDICAP:** You cannot use your hands.
TASK: Walk back and forth across the room 4 times. **HANDICAP:** You must be on your knees.	**TASK:** Walk back and forth across the room 2 times. **HANDICAP:** You must be blindfolded.	**TASK:** Say 5 words to each person in the room. **HANDICAP:** You cannot speak English.
TASK: Pick up 20 pens and put them on a table. **HANDICAP:** You can only use your feet.	**TASK:** Untie the shoelaces of 3 pairs of shoes. **HANDICAP:** You can only use your teeth.	**TASK:** Whistle "Mary Had a Little Lamb" 6 times. **HANDICAP:** You must have 5 soda crackers in your mouth (every time you start).
TASK: Walk around the room twice carrying your Bible. **HANDICAP:** You have to carry it on your head (without using your hands)	**TASK:** Read 2 chapters of the Bible out loud. **HANDICAP:** You must read them backwards (starting with the last verse, ending with the first verse).	**TASK:** Write your name 10 times on a sheet of paper. **HANDICAP:** Your thumbs must be tied together.

Moses: overcoming obstacles and learning to trust

**Read aloud or skim the following Scriptures.
Use what you learn to discuss the related questions.**

Exodus 3:1-12

1 Why do you think God communicated with Moses in such an unusual way?

2 What impact do you think that method of communicating had on Moses' faith?

Reread verses 11 and 12

3 What reason does God give Moses for why he should be the one to lead the people out of Egypt?

4 Does Moses' call (to leadership) have more to do with God or with Moses? Why?

Exodus 3 and 4

5 List all the excuses Moses gave for why he shouldn't do what God asked him to do.

6 Have you ever made excuses to God? What were they?

7 Ask a couple of group members to tell what ended up happening when they made excuses to God.

Skim through the plagues listed in Exodus 8-10

8 Which of these would be the worst for you to endure? Why?

Skim Exodus 11 and 12: 1-14

9 What is the last plague God sends on Egypt.

10 How were the Israelites spared from this plague?

11 What did they have to do to be spared?

12 Why is the event called Passover?

1 Corinthians 5:7

13 Why do you think Paul referred to Jesus as our "Passover lamb" in his letter to the Corinthians?

Exodus 14:5-31

14 How did the Israelites respond to what Pharaoh and his army did after the Israelites left Egypt?

15 How do you think Moses felt at this point?

Exodus 14:13,14

16 What do Moses' words show you about his faith?

17 Had he changed since Exodus 3? If so, how?

18 What effect did this event have on the Israelites' faith? (Check out Exodus 14:31.)

And finally...

19 What events in your life have caused you to increase your trust in God—circumstances, retreats, mission trips, talks you've heard, books you've read?

20 Do you feel you trust God enough? Why/Why not?

SESSION FIVE

JOSHUA & CALEB
BUCKING THE MAJORITY

*Numbers chapter 13
chapter 14*

*Numbers 27:15-20
Joshua 14:13-14*

INTRO

Let's make a deal

Select three students to be contestants on **Let's Make a Deal.** Then send them out of the room. Tell the rest of the group that each contestant must choose between two prizes—one is a five-dollar bill that they can see, and the other is an envelope containing a prize they can't see. Prompt all but two of the students to try to convince the contestants to choose the five-dollar bill. Tell two of the strongest, most spiritually mature student leaders in your group to try to convince the contestants to choose the unknown prize. (None of the students should know what's in the envelopes—just tell them it's a really good prize.) All of them will be yelling advice at the contestants, creating the general chaos that teenagers love.

You'll need...

- *three $5 bills*
- *3 plain sealed envelopes, each containing $10 gift certificates to a cool store (Only 3 of the 6 items will be given away.)*

Invite contestants into the room one at a time, and tell them they get to choose between two prizes. Hold up the money and the envelope, and—while the crowd is yelling at them—tell them they have one minute to make their choice. Give them what they chose, and let them join the crowd to holler at the next contestant.

Segue into your Bible lesson by saying—

The three contestants faced a tough choice: first, whether to go for something they could see or something they couldn't see;

THE LESSON ON
CONFIDENCE

HERE'S THE POINT ▲

A hero is someone who faces a difficult or uncertain situation with strength and confidence.

Joshua and Caleb were heroes. By standing firm in their conviction that they were God's people, they remained confident in the face of opposition. Their confidence qualified them to enter the Promised Land—the only two out of the 12 Jewish undercover agents who did.

How confident is your faith in the midst of opposition? The record of Joshua and Caleb shows that God honors the confidence his people place in him—and he shows himself worthy of our trust.

second, whether to trust the majority of the crowd, which was pressuring them to go with the safest choice, or to trust the two lone voices urging them to go with the scariest choice.

Fresh out of Egyptian slavery, the children of Israel faced the same dilemma. Moses sent 12 spies to scope out the Promised Land. Ten came back, mouths dry and knees weak, cautioning that the inhabitants of Canaan were too big. Their counsel—don't go in. Only two spies said to go for it. Recalling the power God had already shown on Israel's behalf, they tried to convince the people that no opposition was big enough to overthrow God.

The Israelites ultimately listened to the ten fearful spies and chose not to march in and conquer the land. The result? God made sure they had their way. For 40 years the Israelites wandered the desert. The only two who lived to see the promise of God fulfilled were the only two who believed it in the first place—and it's their story we'll look at today.

BIBLE LESSON

Going against the crowd

Your lesson focuses on the passages (primarily in Numbers) concerning the character, confidence, and leadership of Joshua and Caleb. If you are giving a talk, here's a suggested outline:

THE REPORT

📕 Numbers 13

   Summarize the story of the spies exploring Canaan.

   Elaborate on the pressure Joshua and Caleb felt from the crowd of peers and relatives who resisted their confident advice to take the land.

📕 Numbers 13:30
Numbers 14:6-9

   Look at the strength of their faith under pressure. Probe your students for examples of the pressures they face.

   Highlight one or two examples in which students you know have stood firm in their faith in spite of being in the minority.

THE RESULT

 Numbers 14:1-12

Tell the story of the crowd's response to Joshua and Caleb.

Explain how God responded to the crowd

Talk about the times when we rebel against God out of fear or peer pressure. Joshua and Caleb illustrated the value of standing firm in faith.

 Numbers 14:19-30

Make sure kids notice that, although God readily forgave the people when Moses asked him to, their lack of faith kept them from seeing the promises of God fulfilled—they never set foot in the Promised Land. Joshua and Caleb, however, enjoyed the fruit of their confident faith.

THE REWARD

 Numbers 14:24
Numbers 27:15-20
Joshua 14:6-14

Joshua and Caleb were rewarded for their faith by God and ultimately by their own people.

God commended Caleb for his heart full of faith.

God commended Joshua for his leadership.

They were acknowledged by their people, who followed their leadership and gave them a place in Canaan.

Living by faith may be difficult in the short run, but in the long run, it's the only way to truly experience the blessings of God.

SMALL-GROUP DISCUSSION

You'll need...

- *copies of Joshua and Caleb: Going against the Crowd—Small Group Q's 5.1*
- *pencils*
- *extra Bibles*

You know your time frame and your group, so you decide whether to do one or both of the following options. **Going against the Crowd** is straight Bible study, while **Tension Getters** are contemporary versions of Joshua and Caleb's ancient dilemma.

Option 1: Going against the crowd

Here are discussion-starting questions that will drive your kids to the Bible for answers (and even more questions).

Option 2: Tension getters

You'll need...

- *copies of Tension Getters: Going Against the Crowd—Making Connections 5.2*

Form students into three (or more) groups, and give each group one of the **Tension Getters (Making Connections 5.2).**

Each situation presents a dilemma relevant to high school students. In each a teen must stand firm against the crowd. Ask a student in each small group to read aloud their Tension Getter. Then allow a few minutes for each group to talk about what they would do in that situation.

CUSTOM FIT

Is yours the kind of group whose identity is wrapped up in proving a point (however inane that point may be)? Why not make use of all that hot chili pepper by staging a spontaneous, formal debate? Ask each group to read the *same* **Tension Getter** and form an opinion about the right way to deal with the tense situation. Then each group selects a representative to debate the representatives of the other small

APPLICATION

Rate your level of confidence

Ask your students to rate the situations below as you read them. Here's the point of this activity: rating personalizes otherwise hypothetical situations.

Students can get a handle on how confident they are in their faith. They'll leave the session a little clearer about whether or not they are able to stand up against the crowd.

A rating of 1 means it's easy for them to stand up against the crowd; a rating of 6 means it's difficult for them to stand up against the crowd.

Now read the following aloud:

- Everyone around you is cheating on a test you're taking.
- All of your friends are drinking at a party, and they ask you to join them.
- Your friends start gossiping about a friend of yours who isn't present.
- A bunch of your friends are renting hotel rooms on prom night, and they want you to join them.
- The kids in your biology class start talking about evolution and creation. It seems that you are the only one who believes in creation.
- You and your friends are discussing religion. They all believe that since there are many ways to get to God, it doesn't really matter what you believe.

JOSHUA AND CALEB
GOING AGAINST THE CROWD

Read aloud or skim the following Scriptures.
Use what you learn to discuss the related questions.

Numbers 13:17-29

1 After 40 days, the 12 leaders Moses sent to explore the Promised Land return with their report. What do they say?

2 What does their report tell you about them?

Numbers 13:30

3 What does Caleb say about the land?

4 What does that tell you about him?

Numbers 13:31-33

5 What is the difference between the way Caleb talks about the land (verse 30) and the way the rest of the men (except Joshua) talk about the land?

6 What makes the difference in their perspective?

Numbers 14:1-4

7 How do the people respond to the report?

8 Why do you think they respond this way?

9 How would you have responded if you were there?

Numbers 14:6-9

10 Do you think it was hard for Joshua and Caleb stand up to the crowd like they did?

11 Have you ever been in the minority like Joshua and Caleb?

12 What happened?

13 How did you feel?

Numbers 14:10

14 Have you ever been put down or rejected of because of your faith? Do you know someone else who has? Describe the situation.

15 What does the Lord say to Moses about the Israelites?

Numbers 14:11

16 Do you think He had a right to be frustrated? Why/Why not?

17 What does the Lord say about Caleb?

Numbers 14:24

18 What does that tell you about what the Lord wants from us?

19 God forgives the people for rebelling, but what are the consequences of their lack of faith?

Numbers 14:20; 14:29-32

20 How are Joshua and Caleb rewarded for their faith?

21 Judging from this story, how important is our faith?

22 What happens to Joshua and Caleb in the long run?

Numbers 27:15-21; Joshua 14:6-14

23 How is this different from what happened to them at the beginning?

24 What does this tell you about short-term versus long-term results of standing against the crowd?

TENSION GETTERS
GOING AGAINST THE CROWD

Locker Room Chat

Bob and his buddies were clearing out of the locker room after a football game. "So, you meeting Linda again tonight?" asked one of the guys with a grin.

"Don't miss a chance," Bob said as he gave his combination lock one last twist. He smiled, anticipating Linda's welcoming hug. After two years of dating, they enjoyed a close relationship.

"She must be so hot," said another friend.

Bob felt uncomfortable. He didn't answer as he headed for the door.

"You guys sure have been dating a long time. She must be pretty good in bed, huh Bob?"

Bob felt sick. He didn't know what to do. Because Bob was a Christian, he had determined to remain virgin until he was married. He had never told his friends about his decision because he knew they had all had sex. Now he was on the spot.

Should he continue to ignore the comments and walk away, or should he let his friends know about his convictions?

Friday Night Fun

The minute Susan walked into the party, she felt out of place. Her friends had said they were going to the movies, but on the way they decided to go to this party instead. Susan didn't really want to go, but since she wasn't driving there really wasn't much she could say.

When they got to the party, they all started drinking—except for Susan. In fact, she was the only one at the party who didn't drink. Janet, the driver, was drunk by the time they had to leave. None of her other friends seemed to think it was a problem—but then they had been drinking, too.

Susan didn't even have her permit yet, so she couldn't offer to drive. On the other hand, she didn't want to be in the car with Janet at the wheel. Walking home was out—her house was at least five miles away. The only other option was to call her parents for a ride. But then her friends would be busted. Janet turned to Susan and asked, "Are you coming?"

What should Susan do?

Caught in the Act

Tom and some of his friends decided to paint their class year on the driveway at the entrance to their school. Only after they finished the job did one of the guys notice the paint wasn't water-based, but oil-based—permanent! The prank turned out a lot worse than they had planned. At just that moment, a janitor drove in. Tom and his friends ducked behind some bushes. Everyone said if they got caught, they would lie and say they didn't know who did it. Tom didn't say anything. He just prayed they wouldn't be caught.

The next day the janitor reported the incident and said he had seen some guys run away from the scene. Throughout the day, the principal questioned several groups of kids known to hang out with each other—including Tom and his friends.

The principal asked the group point-blank if they knew who had done it. Tom's friends looked at each other like they were annoyed that a bunch of kids would deface school property. They all said *they* didn't know who did it. The principal caught Tom's eye and asked, "Tom, do you know who did this?"

All Tom had to say was no, and he knew the principal would believe him. He was a good student and had never gotten into trouble before. Tom didn't want to lie, but if he told the truth his friends would probably never speak to him again. What should he say?

SESSION SIX

RAHAB
FAITH OVERCOMES A FAST PAST

Joshua 2:1-11
6:13-25
Hebrews 11:31

James 2:25
Matthew 1:5

Those sticky labels

As students come in the room, stick one of the labels on each of their backs. (Be careful about which students get which labels. Don't give a heavy student "too fat," for example.) Don't let them see what label they have been given. Instruct the students to mingle around the room and to treat each other as they would if their labels were really true. (For example, if someone has "too short," another student might say, "Too bad you can't try out for the basketball team" or "Need help getting up on this curb?") Ask the students to guess what label they've been given based on how they are treated by the other students.

You'll need...

- copies of *The Label Mixer—Making Connections 6.1*
- cut out one label for each student
- cellophane tape

Segue into your talk by saying—

> Each of you was given a label that influenced others to treat you a certain way. People regularly give labels to each other. Although the labels you are given are not physically written out, like the ones you had today, they still affect the way you are seen (and treated) by others.

THE LESSON ON
ACTION

HERE'S THE POINT

What you live is what you believe. Everything else is just talk.

The book of James puts it this way: "Faith by itself, if it is not accompanied by action, is dead" (2:17). Many Christians talk the right talk, but God is interested in whether we walk our talk.

Rahab models faith in action. Although her years as a prostitute might seem to disqualify her as a model of faith, Rahab demonstrated that real faith means putting yourself on the line. By faith she chose a path that would change her whole life.

Rahab was labeled by a promiscuous past. Even after she came to know God, she carried the label "prostitute" (see Hebrews 11:31). But through her responsive faith, Rahab rose above her label to take her place among the people of God. Clearly, God saw far beyond her label, for he gave her the privilege of being part of the lineage of Christ!

BIBLE LESSON

Faith in action

Although the story of Rahab is found primarily in the book of Joshua, this lesson also includes New Testament references. Let me warn you right now—you won't have time to do a talk and have a small-group discussion. The **Get Up & Get Moving!** activity for this session takes up too much time. So, what'll it be—the talk or the **Small Group Q's**? If you choose the talk, here's a suggested outline:

RAHAB'S INTRODUCTION

Joshua 2:1-7

When Rahab is first introduced, it is evident that God is already at work in her life—she immediately protected the foreigners against her own people. Why? She had heard about their God (verse 8) and clearly believed in him herself.

She referred to him not as *their* Lord, but *the* Lord (verse 9), acknowledging his sovereignty and power.

She protected the men from her own people because the spies were God's people. Even as a non-Israelite, she had a higher loyalty to the living God.

A contemporary example of loyalty to God superseding loyalty to law is Corrie ten Boom, a Christian living in German-occupied Holland during World War II. Because she hid Jews in her home, she was sent to a concentration camp.

RAHAB'S OPPORTUNITY

Joshua 2:10-11

Rahab made a confession of faith based on what she knew about the Lord.

- Affirm that kids can also confess that God is Lord of all. Coming to faith means acknowledging the saving grace of the Lord and inviting him to become *your* Lord.

- Rahab's faith went beyond confession—her faith became action. She asked the Israelites to take her and her family with them when Israel attacked Jericho.

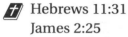 Hebrews 11:31
James 2:25

- Rahab was so convinced that God was real, she was willing to leave her old life behind and begin a new life with the people of God. As a result of her action, her faith is held up as an example to us all.

RAHAB'S REWARD

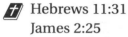 Joshua 6:13-25

- Tell the story of the fall of Jericho.

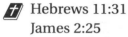 Matthew 1:5

- Explain that Rahab's actions paid off. Not only was Rahab spared, but so was her entire family—and it was because of her faith.

- Rahab's great faith was rewarded even further—she became Salmon's wife (according to Matthew 1:5), which eventually made her the great-grandmother of King David.

- She is one of only five women named in St. Matthew's genealogy of Christ.

- From Rahab's life we can see that putting our faith in action reaps the blessings of being used by God.

CUE TIP

A video clip from *The Hiding Place*, a Christian film about the life of Corrie ten Boom, will say more to kids than even the most stimulating lecture. *Schindler's List*, a more recent film, tells a similar story. In it, Oskar Schindler, a German who defended Jews in World War II, bucks the system for different reasons than ten Boom's.

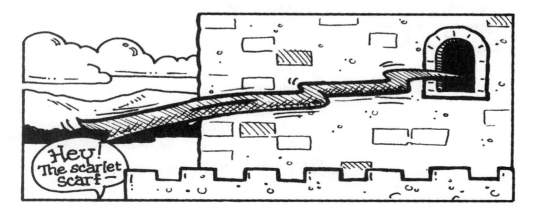

Hey! The scarlet scarf—

GET UP & GET MOVING!

The dating game

You'll need...

- *7 copies of The Dating Game— Script 6.2*
- *wall or divider in the center of the stage*
- *4 chairs placed as illustrated*
- *an applause sign*

Hand out the scripts to your cast ahead of time, and ask them to skim their parts before performing the skit for the group.

SMALL-GROUP DISCUSSION

Your choice...

You'll need...

- *copies of Rahab: Faith in Action!— Small-Group Q's 6.3*
- *pencils*
- *extra Bibles*

I know. You're probably the kind of person who *always* followed directions in school. Most youth workers are (voice heavy with sarcasm). Anyway, just because a Bible lesson *and* a **Small-Group Discussion** *and* a **Get Up & Get Moving!** are all cooked up, so to speak, doesn't mean you have to serve them all to your kids. What I'm saying is, you'll probably do justice to the **Small-Group Discussion** only if you skip the talk. It's up to you.

APPLICATION

Scripture memory

You'll need...

- *card stock*
- *verses printed out on the card stock and cut to 3 x 5 size*
- *a prize*

Print out James 2:14-16 on card stock in such a way that you can cut out 3 x 5 size cards to hand out to students. Offer a prize (to be awarded next week) to any students who memorize these verses.

Or take a look at the next page for a more ambitious—and probably more meaningful—Scripture memory time.

WANT A BIG CHALLENGE?

This requires major planning ahead!

Well before introducing Rahab to your kids, *you* memorize James 2:14-26. Then, when you get to the **Application**, just start saying verse 14 as if it's part of your conversation. (Of course, this presupposes you'd memorize a version that sounded like today's English. *The New Living Translation* or *The Message* works.)

Say—

What's the use of saying that you have faith and are a Christian if you aren't proving it by helping others? Will that kind of faith save anyone?

Then say to one particular student—

Okay, *(student's name)*, **now you ask me that question.**

If they try to use different words, stop them, repeat your quote, and then ask them to try again. Repeat the process with another student or two. Then ask the whole group to repeat the question. Next, quote verses 15-16—and go through the whole thing again.

Once the whole group is saying the three questions with you, tell them they've just memorized James 2:14-16. Then tell them that those who go home with the sheet of paper you're about to hand out and memorize the rest of the passage (through verse 26) will feast on a foot-long, build-your-own sundae at your house after next week's meeting.

THE LABEL MIXER

too short	too tall	too boring	not very smart
bad reputation	a nerd	big flirt	unattractive
bad acne	poor taste in clothes	too quiet	uncoordinated
conceited	too fat	too skinny	a wimp

THE DATING GAME

Cast

Sal Mon, *the bachelor, a devoted man of God in search of a godly woman to marry*
Betty Bible, *Bachelorette Number One, knows the Word of God inside and out*
Donna DoGood, *Bachelorette Number Two, lives a moral life, has never done anything bad*
Rahab Reformed, *Bachelorette Number Three, a shaky past, but now puts her faith in action and lives for God*

Set

Place a wall or divider center stage with one chair on one side and three chairs on the other side—similar to TV's "Dating Game."

HOST:	Welcome to "The Dating Game"! *(applause)* I'm Carolyn Harris *(or your name)*. First, let me introduce you to our bachelorettes. Our first young woman reads the Bible every day and has memorized countless Scripture verses. Let's say hi to Betty Bible! *(applause while Betty comes out and takes her seat, Bible in hand).* Now let's meet Bachelorette Number Two. This young lady is a saint. She spends most of her time at church functions, enjoys socializing with other believers, and never does anything wrong. Let's give a warm welcome to Donna DoGood! *(applause while Donna comes out in a Christian T-shirt)* Our third bachelorette has had a fascinating life. Before she knew God she ran an inn in Jericho. But one day some spies dropped in for a visit—and her life has never been the same since! Please welcome Rahab Reformed! *(applause while Rahab comes out and takes her seat)* Now let's meet our bachelor. This Jewish man says the most important thing in his life is his relationship with God. He's looking for a woman who shares that same passion! His future is very big—his distant descendants will include the Christ himself! Let's give a big "Dating Game" welcome to Sal Mon! *(applause as Sal comes out and takes his seat)* Ladies, why don't you say hello to our bachelor?
BETTY BIBLE:	God loves you, Sal!
DONNA DOGOOD:	Blessings to you, Sal!
RAHAB REFORMED:	Hey, Sal.
HOST:	Okay, Sal, now you've met our bachelorettes. Here are the rules:

you can ask them any questions you want. When the time's up, you must choose one of these lovely bachelorettes to date. And who knows? This bachelorette might just end up as your wife! *(applause)* So let's begin our questions.

SAL:	Bachelorette Number One, how did you come to know God?
BETTY:	Through reading my Bible every day. Romans 3:23 says, "All have sinned and fall short of the glory of God."
DONNA:	I feel sad for those people.
BETTY:	And it goes on to say, "We are justified freely by the grace that came through the redemption of Christ." I'm not sure what it means, but I've memorized it and know that it has something to do with God.
SAL:	Thanks, Bachelorette Number One. Bachelorette Number Two?
DONNA:	I'm so glad you asked. As Betty shared, many people do sin and fall short of the glory of God, which is why I do my best not to. I spend a lot of time at church with my Christian friends, and we try not to do anything wrong.
SAL:	Wow! That must be a challenge.
DONNA:	I'm sure for some people it is. But if you just work hard enough you can do it!
SAL:	Bachelorette Number Three? What about you? How did you come to know God?
RAHAB:	Well, it's kind of a long story. I was…uh, a kind of innkeeper.
DONNA & BETTY:	That's not what <u>we</u> heard!
HOST:	Ladies, you'll have to wait your turn.
RAHAB:	Well, it's true—I've had a bad past. The inn was also a brothel, and to put food on the table for my family I was a prostitute for a while.
DONNA:	*(visibly upset)* Can I switch places with you? I just don't sit next to people like this.
BETTY:	1 John 4:11 says, "Dear friends, since God so loved us, we also ought to love one another." You'd better stay where you are.
RAHAB:	Actually, it's been decades since I was a prostitute. My life dramatically changed when some Israelite spies came and stayed at my home.

SAL:	*(very interested)* Spies? What happened?
RAHAB:	Well, I was living in Jericho at the time, and we kept hearing about the Israelites and how their God was doing great things for them. And when I heard about God, I just knew in my heart that he was real. So the day that some Israelites came to spy out our land, I knew their God was going to do something. I hid the spies in my home because I thought if I helped <u>them</u>. maybe they would help <u>me</u>. Then the city police came to my inn and asked me where the spies were.
SAL:	*(excited)* Sounds like a movie! Exciting!
BETTY:	*(trying to get Sal's attention)* I like to go to movies, Sal!
DONNA:	Me too! As long as they're rated G, that is.
SAL:	Oh, that's nice…Bachelorette Number Three, I'd like to hear more.
RAHAB:	Well, this is where it gets complicated. I knew if the cops found the spies, they'd kill them. So I told the cops that the spies weren't at my house.
DONNA:	You lied? How could you!
BETTY:	"Thou shalt not give false testimony," Exodus 20:16.
RAHAB:	Yeah, I knew it was wrong to lie. But if I told the truth, these men of God would die. I had to decide what was more important. I just knew I had to protect them.
SAL:	So what happened next?
DONNA:	Isn't he supposed to be asking <u>us</u> some questions?
HOST:	Time's almost up Sal. Anything else you want to ask?
SAL:	Yes. Bachelorette Number Three, what happened next?
RAHAB:	After the cops left, I let the spies out the back. I asked them to spare my family's life when they came back to destroy the city, and they agreed. For seven days their people marched around our city. Then on the seventh day, they blew a trumpet and our walls tumbled down. Everything was destroyed. But they kept their promise to come in and get me and my family, and I've been living with them ever since. The best part about it is that through them I came to know God—and my life has never been the same.
HOST:	Okay, Sal, time's up.

page 3

DONNA: But don't I get to share about all the things I <u>haven't</u> done? I don't swear, I don't lie, I don't steal—

BETTY: And I know the Scriptures for all of those things! Wanna hear them?

HOST: Sorry, ladies. Sal, it's time to make your choice.

SAL: It's a tough one, Carolyn. I like that Bachelorette Number One knows the Bible. But the question is, does she live it? And there are many things that Bachelorette Number Two <u>doesn't</u> do. But the question is, what <u>does</u> she do? I know that Bachelorette Number Three has done some things in her past that she's not proud of, but it's clear that God has made a huge difference in her life. That's the kind of woman I'm looking for. I choose Bachelorette Number Three! *(applause)*

HOST: Okay, first meet our other bachelorettes. Betty Bible, come around and say hi to Sal.

BETTY: *(speaks after she comes around the divider and sees Sal)* "Greet one another with a holy kiss," Romans 16:16! *(goes for a kiss from him)*

SAL: Uh, how about a high-five instead? *(they high-five and Betty exits with a bit of a pout)*

HOST: Donna, come and say hi to Sal.

DONNA: *(comes around)* I can't believe you actually chose…<u>that</u> woman. What will people say?

SAL: I don't really care. But thanks for caring. *(Donna exits)*

HOST: Okay, Sal, the big moment is here. Rahab Reformed, come on out and say hi to Sal. *(Rahab comes around)* And let me tell you about your future together. The two of you will date a couple times, get married, and eventually have a son named Boaz! It's kind of a strange thing to name a kid, but he will marry a woman named Ruth. The two of them will be the great-grandparents to a great king named David. He'll do his share of shaky things, but overall he'll be a man after God's own heart. Then after many more generations of marriages and children, the Savior, Jesus Christ, will be born from your lineage. And just think—it all started here on "The Dating Game"! *(applause)* So you two had better be on your way. You've got a lot ahead of you! But first, let's blow the audience that famous Dating Game kiss! Until next week, I'm Carolyn Harris, and this is "The Dating Game"—a place where dreams come true!

END

page 4

SCRIPT 6.2

RAHAB
FAITH IN ACTION!

**Read aloud or skim the following Scriptures.
Use what you learn to discuss the related questions.**

Joshua 2:1-7

1 What did Rahab say to the men who came to her door in search of the spies?

2 Do you think it is right that she did what she did? Why/Why not?

3 When (if at all) is it okay to lie?

Joshua 2:9-11

4 How did Rahab first hear about God?

5 What was her response?

6 Do you see evidence of Rahab's faith in these verses? If so, how?

Joshua 2:12-13

7 What does Rahab's request in these verses tell you about the kind of person she was?

Joshua 6:1-23

8 How did Joshua refer to Rahab?

9 How do you feel about her being referred to this way?

10 How do you think she felt?

Joshua 6:25

11 What happened to Rahab after her life was spared?

12 How do you think her life changed (if at all)?

13 What indications do we have of this in Matthew 1:5?

Skim Hebrews 11

14 How many women are listed in this chapter about faith?

15 What does that tell you about the significance of Rahab's story?

James 2:14-17

16 These verses reveal the relationship between what we believe and how we act. According to this passage, is it possible to believe and not do anything about it? Why/Why not?

James 2:25

17 Rahab was considered righteous for what she did. Do you think she was righteous?

18 Why do you think this verse says that Rahab was considered righteous because of what she did?

SESSION SEVEN

RUTH
KEEPING PROMISES

Ruth chapters 1-5

Agree-disagree

You'll need...

- *two signs: AGREE and DISAGREE*
- *cellophane tape*

Post the two signs, one on each side of the youth room. Read aloud the following statements about commitment. Ask students to show whether they agree or disagree with the statement by standing near the appropriate sign.

1. You are committed to someone when you really enjoy being with them.
2. You are committed to someone when you are related.
3. You are committed to someone when you have a lot of things in common.
4. You are committed to someone when you are dating them.
5. You are committed to someone when you stick with them during tough times.
6. You are committed to someone when you are engaged.
7. You are committed to someone when you are married.
8. You are committed to someone when they are your friend.
9. You are committed to someone when you have known them a long time.
10. You are committed to someone when you make a sacrifice for them.

THE LESSON ON
COMMITMENT

HERE'S THE POINT▲

Commitment means more than saying the right words.

Few people understand the meaning of commitment. Maybe it's because there are so few examples set before us. Broken marriages, distant families, convenient relationships and empty promises corrupt our experience of commitment.

Yet God's Word tells us to honor our commitments—that means learning to live them out. Ruth did just that. She lived out her commitment, even though it included living with her widowed mother-in-law. Her life illustrates the meaning of commitment—and the rewards that come when we are willing to pay the price to stick it out.

Segue into your Bible lesson by saying—

We all have different ideas about what being committed to someone really means. The woman we're talking about today showed what true commitment is all about. Ruth honored her commitments above and beyond what was expected of her.

Think about the commitments you have made. How far are you willing to go to honor a commitment? Would you go as far as Ruth did?

BIBLE LESSON
Ruth reaps more than barley

Although you'll benefit from reading the whole book of Ruth in preparation for your lesson, the actual talk with will focus only on the passages relating to her commitment to Naomi, and on the unforeseen rewards that came to her because of that commitment. Here's a suggested outline for your talk:

RUTH'S PREDICAMENT

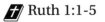 Ruth 1:1-5

- The book of Ruth begins with an Israelite family moving out of the country to escape famine.

- The husband soon died, leaving Naomi and two sons alone in a foreign land.

- As you might expect, the sons married foreign women. In short time, however, both men died, leaving three women without any men to provide for them. (Clue the kids in to the fact that, unlike women in today's society, women who were left alone in those days had no way to support themselves. A woman alone was cared for by her extended family. But of course, having left her extended family in Israel, Naomi had no one but her daughters-in-law.)

- Their troubles created a bond of love among the women.

- Ruth had a choice: make the best of things with Naomi, or return to her own family to be cared for.

RUTH'S RESPONSE

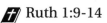 Ruth 1:9-14

- Although both Ruth and her sister-in-law had decided to stay with Naomi, Naomi's decision to return home to Israel was an unsettling surprise to the younger women.

Naomi urged her daughters-in-law to remain in Moab—they were young enough to find new husbands and start a new life.

Both women were devoted to Naomi and grieved their pending separation. Orpah went back to her family, but Ruth's devotion went beyond feelings to lifelong commitment.

Ruth 1:14-17

Honoring the ties of their relationship, Ruth chose to go with Naomi—even though that left her little hope of a second marriage.

As the story continues, it's clear that Ruth's commitment went beyond Naomi to Naomi's God. In staying to help Naomi, Ruth made a lifelong decision to follow God and live among his people.

Our commitments can sometimes have far-reaching effects.

RUTH'S REWARD

Ruth 2:1-3

Ultimately, Ruth was rewarded for her decision, though she could never have predicted God's plans.

Tell a contemporary illustration about how short-term discomfort often leads to long-term rewards.

By honoring the commitment at hand, Ruth ended up in the right place at the right time.

Ruth's chance meeting with Boaz had far-reaching results. Not only did they eventually get married (chapters 2-4), but their son Obed became the grandfather of Israel's King David (Ruth 4:17), and their family is included in the genealogy of Christ (Matthew 1:5).

Ruth 4:14-16

The marriage of Ruth and Boaz brought Naomi new hope and new life, and Ruth's devotion was proclaimed and honored by all.

GET UP & GET MOVING!

Musical masking tape

Tell your students to stand up and mingle while the music is playing, holding their tape sticky side out. Explain that when you stop the music, they must try to stick their tape on someone else before someone sticks their tape on them.

You'll need...

- *masking tape strips at least 1" wide and 3" long*
- *a tape or CD of a song*

The first people to tape someone before getting taped stay in the game for the next round. Those who get taped before taping someone are out. At the end of each round, the students who are still in the game remove their tape from the person on whom they stuck it, and they use the same piece of tape for round two.

Start the music for round two, and repeat the game for at least five rounds. Each time, the students use the same piece of tape they started with. By the end of the game, the tape belonging to the students still playing doesn't stick as well. (If this doesn't happen, move on to the **Small-Group Discussion** and blame the author of this book for the failure of your object lesson. If it does happen, go on to the debrief, and the next day buy five more copies of this fabulous book for your youth worker friends.)

Debrief your group by saying something like this:

> **Did you notice that the first time you stuck your tape on some one, it stuck very well, but the more you removed it and stuck it on others, the less sticky it became?**
>
> **Making commitments is a lot like that. The more we stick with our commitments, the stronger our commitments are. But the more times we back out on a commitment, the more likely we are to skip out on other commitments—we simply haven't developed the discipline to stick with our promises.**
>
> **Although sticking with a commitment isn't easy—Ruth's story shows that—in the long run, staying with our commitments brings great joy. When early in life we develop the discipline of honoring our relatively easy commitments, we will be strong enough in our later life to stick to our more demanding commitments.**

SMALL-GROUP DISCUSSION
Rewards of commitment

Form small groups of students to discuss the questions on the worksheet. Pick and choose only a few **Q's** if you are short on time.

You'll need...

- copies of *Ruth: The Rewards of Commitment— Small Group Q's 7.1*
- pencils
- extra Bibles

APPLICATION
Personal-time survey

Ask students to write down in the second column how much time they spend doing the activities listed in the first column. (Remind them there are only 24 hours in a day, so their activities can't total more than that. That's a good thing for you to remember, too!)

You'll need...

- copies of *The Time Survey—Making Connections, 7.2*
- pencils
- cellophane tape

Before the fast thinkers get restless, tell the kids to circle those activities in which they spend the most time. Then ask them to note that the way they spend their time reveals what they are committed to.

Now ask them to mark in the third column the amount of time they would *like* to spend doing the activities listed. They can either post their sheets somewhere in their room to remind them of their time commitment goals, or simply take them home and post them there.

Ruth
THE REWARDS OF COMMITMENT

Read aloud or skim the following Scriptures.
Use what you learn to discuss the related questions.

Ruth 1:1-7

1   List all the tragic circumstances that happened at the beginning of the book of Ruth.

2   Which tragedy would have been the hardest for you if you were Naomi?

3   Do you think Ruth and Orpah had any obligation to Naomi? Why or why not?

Ruth 1:8-18

4   How did the daughters-in-law initially respond to Naomi's suggestion that they return to their childhood homes?

5   What did Orpah eventually do? What about Ruth?

6   Do you think you would have responded more like Orpah or more like Ruth? Why?

7   What reasons did Ruth have for leaving Naomi? For staying with Naomi? Why do you think she chose as she did?

8   Have you ever made a sacrifice for someone because you were committed to them? If so, what was it? If not, why not?

Ruth 2:3

9   After Ruth and Naomi arrived in Bethlehem, Ruth went to glean in the fields for food. At whose field did she end up?

10   Do you think this was just a coincidence? Why or why not?

Ruth 2:5-12

11   What happened between Ruth and Boaz?

12   How was Ruth rewarded for her commitment to Naomi?

13   How do you think Boaz heard about what Ruth had done for Naomi?

Ruth 4:11; 5:22

14   When Boaz eventually announced that he would marry Ruth, the elders gave him a blessing. How did this blessing come true?

Matthew 1:5

15   What happened to Naomi as a result of Ruth's marriage?

16   How many people were affected (directly or indirectly) by Ruth's commitment to Naomi?

Ruth 4:14-17

17   In your opinion, how much of an impact does keeping (or breaking) our commitments have on other people?

18   How has your life been affected by people who have kept (or broken) a commitment to you?

19   How have you affected others by the keeping or breaking of your own commitments?

20   On a scale of 1 to 10, how committed are you as a person? (1 being utterly *un*committed, and 10 being extremely committed)

21   How committed would you *like* to be?

THE TIME SURVEY

ACTIVITIES	HOW MUCH TIME I SPEND	HOW MUCH TIME I'D LIKE TO SPEND
sleeping		
eating		
talking on the phone		
watching T.V.		
surfing the Internet		
doing homework		
going to school		
exercising		
talking to parents		
reading the Bible		
playing sports		
praying		
school activities		
church activities		
spending time with boyfriend/girlfriend		
spending time with friends		
other (anything not mentioned)		

SESSION EIGHT

DAVID
TRUTH HURTS LESS THAN LIES

2 Samuel chapters 11 and 12
Psalm 51:1-12

INTRO

Guess who's telling the truth

Be looking for the arrival of two students you think could lie well. (All right, stop thinking "What? Just two?") Invite to the front a third student—someone who's done something unusual, adventurous, risky, or embarrassing. Also invite up the two others you've picked out. Explain to all three in front of the group that they will all try their best to convince the crowd that they are the one who has done this certain unusual activity. The audience knows only one of them is telling the truth, but they don't know which one.

You'll need...

- *to talk ahead of time to a student who has done something unusual—and make sure she'll be at this session*

Begin by having all three students say what they've done in the same, already composed, concise statement. (For example, one after the other, the three students say, "I went bungee jumping when I was 16.") The audience then asks questions of the three students to determine which one is telling the truth. (Encourage the audience to ask for details rather than just variations of "Did you really do this?")

After all three students have answered some questions, tell the audience it's time to vote on which student is telling the truth. Give a prize to the student who gets the most votes.

Our lies shield us from our true selves.

It doesn't matter whether the lie is spoken outright or merely something we decide to keep secret. Either way, lies keep us from dealing with the truth. Yet it's only in facing the truth that we find freedom.

David was a godly man caught in a secret sin. With the help of the prophet Nathan, he learned that the only way to free himself from lies was to confess them. David's story affirms that healing comes through confession— and only the truth can set us free.

Segue into your Bible lesson by saying—

> Sometimes it's hard to tell what the truth really is. We just had to choose the student who seemed the most convincing. But three people in the room knew the truth down deep inside. While they were answering questions, they knew whether they were lying or telling the truth.
>
> At times it's difficult to tell the truth—usually because we're ashamed or afraid. The problem is, our lies don't ever solve the problem or make it go away. They usually just make things worse.
>
> David found this out when he tried to hide his sin. He thought that if no one knew about it, it would just go away. But it didn't. As we look at his story, think about the lies you've told (or the information you've withheld). Did the lies make your situation better or worse?

BIBLE LESSON

Sex, lies—and repentance

David did many acts that showed what a godly, heroic person he was. Most likely, however, no action taught him more than his sin with Bathsheba. Your lesson focuses on the circumstances that snared King David into adultery and murder. It also traces his path through the lies to the confession that finally set him free. Here's a suggested outline for your talk:

DAVID'S FALL

2 Samuel 11:1

David's first mistake was staying home when it was the time for kings to go off to war. Instead of fighting a war, he became bored and restless at home. We more easily fall into temptation when we are in the wrong place at the wrong time.

David's temptation occurred in three stages:
1. From his palace rooftop, he saw Bathsheba bathing.
2. Instead of turning away, he sent someone to inquire about her.
3. Instead of honoring Bathsheba's marriage, David sent for her to come to him.

At any one of these stages David could have stopped, but he just kept going. The power of the temptation increased every time he gave in to his desires.

Contrast David's actions in this passage with Joseph's actions in Genesis 39. David lingered while Joseph fled—and that made all the difference.

DAVID'S COVER-UP

2 Samuel 11:6-13

When David found out that Bathsheba was pregnant, he immediately tried to cover up his actions instead of confessing his sin.

David called home Uriah, Bathsheba's husband, from the battle lines and urged him to go sleep with Bathsheba.

Uriah, unwilling to enjoy pleasure while his fellow soldiers risked their lives, slept on the palace patio and foiled David's plan.

The next night David got Uriah drunk and once again urged him to go home to Bathsheba. Uriah spent a second night on the patio.

In desperation, David arranged to have Uriah placed on the front lines so he would be killed in battle.

Once Uriah was out of the way, David took Bathsheba to be his wife. He thought he had it made, but God wasn't fooled.

DAVID'S FREEDOM

2 Samuel 12:1-14

One can only imagine how David felt in his heart being the only one (besides Bathsheba) who knew the truth about what he had done.

But God loved David too much to let him get away with it. God sent the prophet Nathan to confront David.

David's response to Nathan's incriminating story showed that David fully understood and hated injustice. When it came to judging his own injustice, however, he was blinded by the powerful denial that settles over the heart of the liar.

When Nathan said, "You are the man," he offered David freedom from his sin by confronting him directly.

Psalm 51:1-12

David snapped out of his denial and immediately responded by admitting his sin and accepting the consequences.

Though he could never undo the pain and death caused by his lie, David received forgiveness from God—and he experienced the freedom that comes with facing the truth.

God showed his incredible capacity to bless and forgive by giving David and Bathsheba another son, Solomon, who was a direct ancestor of Christ.

SMALL-GROUP DISCUSSION

Truth or consequences

Form small groups among your students. After they discuss the **Small-Group Q's**, kids should stay in their small groups for **Two Truth's and a Lie.**

You'll need...

- copies of **David: Truth or Consequences — Small Group Q's 8.1**
- pencils
- extra Bibles

GET UP & GET MOVING!

Two truths and a lie

Play this version of the game in small groups so everyone has a chance to participate. And read the instructions all the way through—there's a twist on the usual game rules.

Every group member writes down three statements about themselves—two that are true and one that's a lie. Explain that, since they get points based on whether or not they fool the rest of the group with their statements, they should state unusual things they've done, places they've been, or things that have happened to them. What you don't tell them is how they get those points. Ask the group leader to keep track of the points without letting the kids in their group know how the point system works.

One at a time, each person in the group reads all three of their statements. Then the rest of the group votes on which statement they think is a lie. The point system goes like this:

- If the person fools everyone, he gets only 1 point.
- If the person fools only some people—2 points.
- If the person doesn't fool anyone—3 points.
- Everyone in the group who guesses correctly which one is the lie gets 5 points.

When the game is over, explain the point system and announce the winner. Surprise! The winners are the ones who best tell and discern the truth—not the ones who are the best liars.

Debrief your group by saying something like this—

> **You probably expected the winners to be the best liars—which, actually, is too often true. Doesn't everybody know that if you tell the truth about something you've done wrong, you'll just get in trouble? And that if you lie about it, you're off the hook?**
>
> **In reality, though, the longer we avoid telling the truth, the more trouble we bring on ourselves. You were rewarded in this game for being a bad liar because God *wants* us to be bad liars. He wants us to excel at telling the truth.**

You'll need...

- *copies of **Psalm 51— Making Connections 8.2***
- *pencils*

Hand out to each student a copy of Psalm 51. Instruct them to write their own paraphrase of this psalm as a prayer of confession. Give them the option of sharing their paraphrase with the rest of their group or of keeping it to themselves. If you have time, let students find private places to complete this exercise by themselves.

DAVID
TRUTH OR CONSEQUENCES

**Read aloud or skim the following Scriptures.
Use what you learn to discuss the related questions.**

2 Samuel 11:1

1   Was David where he was supposed to be? Why or why not?

2 Samuel 11:2-5

2   As a group, list all the mistakes David made.

3   Where in David's experience do you think it would have been easiest for him to stop and avoid falling into temptation?

4   Where do you think it became too difficult (or tempting) for him to stop?

5   The more David kept going, the harder it was for him to stop. Do you find this to be true when you are being tempted? Why or why not?

6   In what situations have you been tempted? If you avoided the temptation, how did you do it? If you fell into temptation, how did it happen?

2 Samuel 11:6-13

7   After David fell, he immediately tried to cover it up. Have you ever tried to cover something up? What happened? (Anyone want to share their experience?)

2 Samuel 11:14-17

8   Eventually, David had Uriah put on the front lines so he would be struck down and killed. How responsible was David for Uriah's death?

9   How do you think David got to the point where he could order a friend to be murdered?

10   Do you think he was evil or desperate or both?

11   In what ways can you relate to David's feelings?

2 Samuel 11:18-27

12   Did David get away with what he did? Why or why not?

2 Samuel 12:1-7

13   What does David's response to Nathan's story tell you about David?

2 Samuel 12: 7-12

14   How do you think David felt when Nathan told him the truth about what he did? How would you have felt?

15   Do you think David's night of passion was worth it? Why or why not?

2 Samuel 12: 24

16   Ultimately, God restores David and even blesses him with a second son with Bathsheba. What does this tell you about God's forgiveness?

And finally...

17   After reading David's story, do you think there's anything God doesn't forgive? What do we have to do to experience God's forgiveness?

PSALM 51

verses 1-12

King David's version   **My version**

Have mercy on me, O God,
According to your unfailing love;
According to your great compassion
Blot out my transgressions.

Wash away all my iniquity
And cleanse me from my sin.
For I know my transgressions,
And my sin is always before me.

Against you, you only, have I sinned
And done what is evil in your sight,
So that you are proved right when
        you speak
And justified when you judge.

Surely I was sinful at birth,
Sinful from the time my mother
        conceived me.
Surely you desire truth in the inner
        parts;
You teach me wisdom in the inmost
        place.

Cleanse me with hyssop, and I will
        be clean;
Wash me and I will be whiter than
        snow.
Let me hear joy and gladness;
Let the bones you have crushed
        rejoice.

Hide your face from my sins
And blot out all my iniquity.
Create in me a pure heart, O God,
And renew a steadfast spirit within
        me.

Do not cast me from your presence
Or take your Holy Spirit from me.
Restore to me the joy of your
        salvation
And grant me a willing spirit, to
        sustain me.

SESSION NINE

ESTHER
RIGHT WOMAN, RIGHT PLACE, RIGHT TIME

Esther 2:1-18
3:1-11
4:1-17

Esther 5:1-8
7:1-10

HERE'S THE POINT

God has created each one of us for a purpose.

Many people struggle to discover the unique purpose for which they are made. Somewhere between our circumstances and our choices, we usually discover our purpose in life. The secret to finding purpose is using what we've been given to serve God and benefit others.

The book of Esther teaches us that the greatest purpose for our lives is found right in the middle of our circumstances. But it may take great courage to live it out.

INTRO

Royalty for a day

Read the questions below, then adjust the prizes to fit your youth group. Before kids come into your room, place three chairs up front to be your thrones. Put stickers underneath each of the remaining chairs, three of which have crowns marked on them.

Once all the students sit down, tell them to look under their chairs for their stickers. The people who have crowns on their stickers are the royalty. They come to the front of the room and sit on the thrones. Promptly serve them donuts and juice—no one else gets any. Ask each of them one of the following questions concerning what they will do during their "reign":

You'll need...

- *3 chairs*
- *stickers for all students (draw crowns on 3 of them)*
- *3 prizes (see the 3 questions below)*

1. **You may have a full scholarship to our next youth group event—or you may give everyone in the group $5 off the event. Which do you choose?**
2. **You may keep a whole book of coupons for free ice cream, or you may give everyone in the group one coupon each. Which do you choose?**

3. You may have a free dinner at a nice restaurant in town, or you may order free pizza for everyone in the group. Which do you choose?

Make sure the students receive whatever they chose.

Debrief your group by asking your royalty the following questions:

- How did it feel to be put in that position? Did you like the feeling? Why or why not?

- Why did you choose the way you did? Was it a hard decision or an easy decision? Why?

Segue into your talk by saying—

At first our royalty seemed to be the luckiest ones in the room. But then they had to make a difficult choice. They had to decide whether to hold on to what they were given or to use it for the well-being of others. Esther faced the same choice. We're going to look at her story now.

BIBLE LESSON AND GET UP & GET MOVING!

Princess bride, national savior

Your students will tell the story of Esther through art and drama.

Ask your students to form groups of four or more. (If you have fewer than 20 students, double up on the passages and have fewer groups. If you have a lot of students, appoint leaders to facilitate the groups). Each group chooses one of the passages listed below, reads it, and figures out how they'll communicate the main idea (or story line) of their passage to the rest of the youth group. Half of each group works on creating a poster that illustrates the passage; the other half comes up with a "minute mime" (a one-minute drama without words) to act out the passage.

You'll need...

- *colored pens or crayons*
- *5 poster boards*

Here are the five passages:
- Esther 2:1-11, 17-18
- Esther 3:1-6, 8-11
- Esther 4:1-17
- Esther 5:1-8
- Esther 7:1-10

Give each group 10 to 15 minutes to read the passage, create a mime, and illustrate a poster board. Then bring the groups together to share their creative renditions (in the order above). Each group leaves its poster board up front, providing a visual summary of the story of Esther.

Remembering who you are

- copies of *Esther: Remembering Who You Are— Small Group Q's 9.1*
- pencils
- extra Bibles

Use this lesson's **Small Group Q's 9.1** to fill out the details of the summarized story as it was presented in the the **Bible Lesson** above.

APPLICATION

You'll need...

- copies of *How Are You Living God's Purpose in Your Life?—Making Connections 9.2*
- pencils
- extra Bibles

CUSTOM FIT

Hey, try this. Instead of shifting to new groups for the discussion to follow, leave your students in the five groups they formed for the Bible Lesson—unless those groups were too small or too large for effective discussion to occur. Small groups of three to eight students work best.

After handing out the worksheets, allow your students about five minutes to reflect on their lives and check one of the three responses in each box that describes them. (If you have run out of time, send it home with them.)

ESTHER
REMEMBERING WHO YOU ARE

**Read aloud or skim the following Scriptures.
Use what you learn to discuss the related questions.**

To begin...

1 Make two columns on the back of this sheet, like this:

THINGS WE ARE GIVEN   THINGS WE CHOOSE

As a group, list in the first column what life simply gives us that we don't get to choose—family, appearance, etc. In the second column, list some things in life that we *do* get to choose—friends, school clubs, etc.

Esther 2:1-17

2 Did Esther become queen because of something she was given or because of something she did?

3 How much do you think God was involved in her becoming queen?

Esther 3:1-11

4 What were Haman's motives for asking the king to have the Jews destroyed?

5 What does this passage tell you about Haman? About the king?

Esther 4:1-9

6 After the king's edict, what did Mordecai ask Esther to do?

7 Was this an easy request for Esther to fulfill? Why or why not?

Esther 4:12-14

8 Do you think it was fair for Mordecai to put Esther under such pressure? Why/Why not?

9 Before reading any farther, list on the back of this sheet all the options Esther had at this point in her story.

Esther 4:15,16

10 Now look at her response. Do you think it was her responsibility to respond the way she did?

11 If you were in her place, do you think you would have done the same thing?

And finally...

12 Think back to our "Royalty for a Day" game. How is Esther's story similar to what happened to the kings and queens in the group?

13 Have you ever felt scared to do what God wanted you to do? Can you tell your small group the details?

14 Do you think we're supposed to let God use everything in our life for his glory? If so, are you living this way? If not, what needs to change for this to happen?

SESSION TEN

JOB
BAD DAYS FOR GOOD PEOPLE

Job chapters 1-2
chapter 4
chapter 8
chapter 15

Job chapter 32
chapters 38-41
42:1-7

Would you rather...?

Ask your students the following questions, and have them vote on which experience they'd rather have happen to them.

Would you rather:
• Suffer and be wise or be happy and ignorant?
• Lose everything and get back twice as much or keep everything you have now?
• Live comfortably and be shallow or go through pain and be deep?
• Have friends that give bad advice or have no friends at all?
• Die with your family or live alone?
• Lose your wealth or lose your integrity?
• Have painful sores all over your body or be put out of your misery and die?
• Be married to someone who mocks you or not be married at all?
• Give in to the devil and be happy or stand firm against the devil and be in pain?
• Get answers from friends or get answers from God?

Segue into your talk by saying—

> Most of you are probably thankful you don't have to choose any of the options I just gave you. But these were Job's options—

Suffering may be the condition from which humans benefit the most.

When you suffer, you feel rejected. Even, sometimes, by God. Yet just the opposite may be true. Some of the pain you suffer in life is actually God's honoring you. It means he's drawing you near to himself. Face it—too often we turn to God only when things are so tough that we have nowhere left to turn.

Job was a servant of God who learned to turn to God during suffering. When the bottom dropped out, he couldn't find help in his circumstances, his family, or his friends. In the end he found his help in God. And that made all the difference.

Get kids to show their preferences by some sort of action. For instance, designate one side of the room as the place to stand if they vote for the first option, and the other side of the room for the other option. Or tell them to stand up if they want option one and stay seated if they want option two.

For more "Would you rather...?" questions, check out *Would You Rather...?* by Doug Fields, and— by Les Christie—*What If...?* and *Have You Ever...?* (all published by Youth Specialties). They'll get your kids talking (especially during long van rides).

only they weren't optional. One of those things in each pair just happened to him—unasked for.

Think about the pain you've experienced in the context of Job's experience. While discovering Job's story, look for ways you can, like Job, embrace the blessings found only in the wounds.

BIBLE LESSON

Ouch—this hurts

You'll need...

- *index cards*
- *pencils*

Before you begin your talk, pass out an index card to each of your students. Give them a minute to think of the most painful experience they've ever had. Ask them to write their name and a short description of their experience on the card.

Tell them they must turn in their index cards to you at the end of your talk. Warn them that you'll be reading each one out loud, though without identifying the writers. Your group will then vote on which experience they think is the worst. That person will receive the Suffering Servant Award.

Although the story of Job is 42 chapters long, your lesson focuses only on select passages that summarize the main idea of the story. Here's your outline:

JOB'S CIRCUMSTANCES

📖 Job chapters 1 and 2

🏃 Of all the tragedies that happened to Job, not one of them was his fault. They were circumstances that Satan arranged and that God allowed.

🏃 We are let in on the behind-the-scenes interaction between God and Satan. From our insider view we learn of the spiritual dimension of Job's troubles. Job, on the other hand, was clueless. For all he knew, he had been abandoned by God.

🏃 Even so, Job did not curse God for what happened (Job 1:22, 2:10). He accepted his circumstances even though he didn't understand what was going on.

JOB'S COMPANIONS

🏃 Job's companions tried to make him feel better by telling him what to do.

🏃 Job's wife (2:9)
1. She often gets a bad rap for her obvious bitterness.

2. Remember, though, that all her children had just been killed by a natural disaster. In the depths of her grief, she questioned a God who allowed innocent people to suffer.
3. Many people react to suffering like Job's wife did: with bitterness.

📖 Job chapter 4
   chapter 8
   chapter 15
   chapter 32

🚶 Job's three friends (Job 2:12,13)
1. Although they started out very well, sitting with Job, crying with him, and not saying a word, things went downhill when they opened their mouths.
2. Highlight a few of their comments, and remind kids that much of what they say isn't wrong—it's just that their comments don't apply to Job's situation.
3. We all make some heinous mistakes in trying be a friend, like listening too little and talking too much, thinking we know exactly how our friend feels, or trying to fix situations with pat answers.

JOB'S CONFRONTATION

🚶 Ultimately, Job stops listening to his friends and starts listening to God.

🚶 How often do we get to that point? Most of the time, we take our pain to others, hoping they have the words to make us feel better.

🚶 Job shows us that our best bet is to take our pain to God.

📖 Job chapters 38-41

🚶 God answers Job by questioning him. Through God's questions, Job finds the perspective he needs.

📖 Job 42:1-6

🚶 Job's response in the last chapter shows that he understood his pain in a new way.

🚶 God had been faithful in giving Job the answers he needed.

📖 Job 42:7

🚶 The irony of Job's offering a sacrifice to God for his friends' misunderstanding shows that people who appear to have all the right answers can't always be trusted.

🚶 Ultimately, we shouldn't assume people who suffer are being punished by God. It might be they're being honored by him—being counted worthy to bear the pain.

Now collect all the cards that describe the difficult circumstances your students have been through.

Without reading any names, read the situations out loud to your group. Have the students vote on which situation they think is the hardest or most painful. Call up to the front the student who wrote about that experience and give her the Suffering Servant Award.

As you are giving the student her prize, make the connection back to Job by saying something like this—

> **Usually, we are pitied for our pain. But Job shows us that in God's opinion we should be honored for bearing up under painful circumstances. Therefore, we give this award today to the person who has been through the most pain as a reminder to us that suffering is not always bad.**
>
> **Instead of running from our pain, may we let it do its work in our lives.**

SMALL-GROUP DISCUSSION

Tried but true

You'll need...

- copies of **Job: Tried But True—Small Group Q's 10.1**
- pencils
- extra Bibles

The handout contains discussion-starting questions that will drive your kids to the Bible for answers (and even more questions).

APPLICATION

Quit talking for once and listen

You'll need...

- copies of **The Message of Job— Making Connections 10.2**
- pencils

The **Making Connections** worksheet is Job 42:2-6 in *The Message*—a contemporary-language translation of parts of the Bible. Pass it out and ask a student to read it aloud. Tell students to list on their sheets all the things Job learned from his experience of suffering. Then give them a few quiet moments to circle the lessons that are most significant to them right now.

Eugene Peterson's *The Message* now includes the New Testament and the book of Job (NavPress, 1996). Pick one up, being the suffering servant you are. After all, you work with teenagers—and in your pain, you are honored. (The day you start cutting yourself with pottery, however, means it's probably time to find a new church.)

Job: tried but true

Read aloud or skim the following Scriptures.
Use what you learn to discuss the related questions.

1   As a group, make a list on the back of this sheet of all the things that cause people to suffer.

2   Do you think God allows suffering because he's punishing us? Why or why not?

Job 1:1-19

3   Why did God allow Job to suffer?

4   Do you think God was unfair? How do you think Job felt?

Job 2:1-10

5   What do you think Job thought when he was sitting among the ashes? Have you ever felt this way? What did you do?

6   Why do you think Job's wife's was so bitter?

7   Do you know any bitter people? What causes them to feel that way?

Job 2:11-13

8   When you were there for a friend who was going through a hard time, what did you do or say (if anything)? How did your friend respond to you?

9   Did you feel good about the way you supported them? (Have the group share their experiences.)

Read Job's first words in Job 3

10   Have you ever been this depressed? If so, what did you do (if anything) to feel better? What finally made you feel better?

Job 4:6-8

11   What did Eliphaz say to comfort Job? Do you think his advice was helpful?

Job 8:4-6

12   What did Bildad say? Was it helpful?

Job 11:14-17

13   How about Zophar?

Job 16:1-2

14   Have your friends ever comforted you with words that didn't really help? How did it make you feel?

15   Can you relate to Job's response to his friends?

Job chapter 31

16   Have you ever been mad enough at God to lay out your case before him the way Job did? If not, why not? If so, what did you do?

Job chapters 38-42:7

17   Although God answered Job by asserting his authority as Creator, do you get the feeling that he was angry with Job for questioning him?

Job 42:10-16

18   What happened to Job in the end?

Job 42: 1-6

19   How did his perspective change in the process?

20   What does all this teach you about your relationship with God?

Job

Read the Scripture below from the book of Job. In the space below the Bible passage, list the things Job learned from his experience, based on this Scripture.

JOB ANSWERED GOD:

"I'm convinced: You can do anything and everything.
　　　Nothing and no one can upset your plans.
You asked, 'Who is this muddying the water,
　　　Ignorantly confusing the issue, second-guessing my purposes?'
I admit it. I was the one. I babbled on about things far beyond me,
　　　Made small talk about wonders way over my head.
You told me, 'Listen, and let me do the talking.
　　　Let me ask the questions. You give the answers.'
I admit I once lived by rumors of you;
　　　Now I have it all firsthand—from my own eyes and ears!
I'm sorry—forgive me. I'll never do that again, I promise!
　　　I'll never again live on crusts of hearsay, crumbs of rumor."

—from Eugene Peterson's *The Message: Job*

THINGS JOB LEARNED FROM HIS EXPERIENCE:

SESSION ELEVEN

DANIEL
NO FEAR

Daniel chapters 1-6

INTRO

Sharks and minnows

Appoint one student to be the shark; the rest are minnows. The shark stands in the middle of the room, and all of the minnows stand on one side. The

You'll need...

- *no materials*

object of the game is for the minnows to run to the other side of the room without getting tagged by the shark. Any students who get tagged become sharks. Go several rounds until there are only a few minnows left. Punch up the energy by offering prizes.

Segue into your Bible lesson by saying—

> **In this game you discovered that the only way to win was to go toward the sharks. The longer you stayed on the side lines (and didn't run), the more likely it was that you got caught. You had to beat them by jumping in and running fast. Hesitating and going slow left you vulnerable.**
>
> **That same strategy works to help us beat our fears and develop courage in life. The only way to be courageous is to act courageous. Over time you discover that you actually *are* less and less afraid.**
>
> **Daniel lived his faith courageously. As we look at his story, think about what stops you from living out your own faith with courage. Explore Daniel's life to find what his story can teach you about developing courage.**

THE LESSON ON

COURAGE

HERE'S THE POINT ▲

Courage grows as it is acted upon.

Like a muscle, the more we use courage, the bigger it gets. The more we ignore courage, the smaller it becomes.

Courage is a trait worth developing in our faith, as Daniel proved when he followed God with courage. His story is a testimony to what can happen when we boldly put our life in God's hands.

"All men die, but not all men really live," said Mel Gibson's character in the movie *Braveheart*. Daniel knew what it meant to live.

BIBLE LESSON

He feared compromise more than death

Although the book of Daniel is 12 chapters long, your lesson will focus only on the passages that demonstrate Daniel's courage. Here is a suggested outline:

DANIEL'S DISCIPLINE

📖 Daniel chapter 1

- Daniel was a disciplined man (verse 8)—a trait necessary for developing courage.

- With all the opportunities for indulgence at the palace, Daniel and his friends had to discipline themselves.

- It's helpful to have our friends' support when we are trying to develop discipline in our lives. Daniel was not alone.

- By staying strong right from the start, Daniel was developing the discipline he needed to be strong in the days ahead.

DANIEL'S REWARD

📖 Daniel 1:15-17

- Through his discipline, Daniel became strong in mind and body (Daniel 1:15-17).

- Too much food, alcohol, TV, or laziness clouds our minds and keeps us from being controlled by the Holy Spirit.

- Daniel's discipline kept his head clearer to be able to hear the Lord.

📖 Daniel chapters 2-5

- Listening for God was the secret of his ability to interpret dreams

- He was elevated to a position of power and influence because of his dependence on God.

DANIEL'S CONSISTENCY

📖 Daniel 2:23
4:2-3

- Even though Daniel was in a position of power, he never stopped leaning on God.

He knew God was the source of his knowledge and ability

📖 Daniel 2:47
4:34-35

Because of Daniel's faith, kings came to recognize the power of God as well.

📖 Daniel 6:3-4

Others grew jealous of Daniel's power and his influence with the kings. They tried to trap Daniel with a decree that said he had to worship King Darius instead of God. But Daniel remained faithful to God as he had always done before, and he trusted God with the outcome.

📖 Daniel 6:16-22

The consistency of Daniel's life gave him the courage he needed to face whatever lay ahead—and God met him every step of the way. Even in a lion's den!

GET UP & GET MOVING!

Who you gonna listen to?

Well ahead of the session during which you run this skit, cast six students for "Which Voice Do You Listen to?" Provide each participant with a script, asking each one to practice on their own before the next youth group session.

You'll need...

- *7 copies of the script* **Which Voice Do You Listen To?—Script 11.1**

After they've performed the skit for the group, debrief everyone with the following questions:

- **Have you ever experienced what Chris experienced in this skit? Which of the three situations did you relate to the most?**
- **How do you think Chris felt at the end of the skit? Have you ever felt this way?**
- **Do you think Chris would have been more courageous if he started out being up front about his faith? Why/Why not?**
- **Based on what you've learned about Daniel, how do you think he would have responded if he were in Chris's place?**
- **When you face challenges in your faith, are you more inclined to follow the voice of Captain Courage or Captain Coward?**
- **In which situations is it hardest for you to live by faith?**

PLAN AHEAD

FOR THIS ONE

This skit works better if your students practice it ahead of time.

SAVE IT!

If you played Sharks and Minnows, taught the **Bible Lesson**, and did the skit and follow-up questions, you probably don't have time for **Small-Group Discussion** — unless you're a marathon youth leader who captivates kids in Bible lessons for hours on end.

Those of you in the real world, however, will probably want to save the small-group questions for another time.

SMALL-GROUP DISCUSSION

No fear

You'll need...

- copies of *Daniel: No Fear—Small Group Q's 11.2*
- *pencils*
- *extra Bibles*

Form small groups among your kids. Send them to different corners of the room with the **Small Group Q's.**

APPLICATION

Chart your courage

Hand out one chart to each student. Challenge them to track their courage for one week. Before they go to bed each night, they are to record what happened that day and give themselves a score (from 1-10) on the courage monitor. Invite students to bring their courage charts back next week and share their results in their small groups.

You'll need...

- copies of *Courage Chart —Making Connections 11.3*

WHICH VOICE
DO YOU LISTEN TO?

CAST

Chris, Christian guy
Captain Courage, girl or guy
Captain Coward, girl or guy
Freddie, guy
Dan, guy
Mrs. Young, girl

SET

Scene 1: no props
Scene 2: 3 chairs and a desk (a classroom look)
 3 pieces of paper and 3 pens.

Scene 1
On the way to class

FREDDIE: Man, what a weekend. That party was so hot.

DAN: Yeah, but you probably don't remember most of it. You were so wasted!

FREDDIE: I know. I had the biggest headache Sunday morning. I told my mom I thought I had the flu, and stayed I bed all day. But it was worth it! It was a great party. Hey, whatever happened with you and Monica?

DAN: Some things you just shouldn't talk about! *(they both laugh)*

FREDDIE: Hey, Chris! What did you do this weekend?

 (Courage and Captain Coward pop out on either side of Chris. They are invisible to Dan and Freddie. While they speak, Chris appears as if he's lost in thought.)

CAPTAIN COURAGE: Chris, this is your chance! Tell them about the camp.

CAPTAIN COWARD:	Are you crazy? These guys are going to think you're the biggest loser in the world if you tell them that.
CAPTAIN COURAGE:	No, Chris. Deep down inside, these guys need God too. If you step out and take a risk and tell them you're a Christian, it might open up a conversation that could eventually lead them to God!
CAPTAIN COWARD:	No way, Chris. These guys will never be interested in God. If you bring that part of your life into the picture, they'll dump you as a friend. Don't do it. Play it safe.
DAN:	*(interrupting Chris's trance)* Chris, Freddie just asked you what you did this weekend.
CHRIS:	*(coming to from his thoughts)* Oh, I'm sorry. I—uh—I went to the mountains.
FREDDIE:	That's cool. Did you go skiing?
CHRIS:	Not exactly. I went away with some friends.
DAN:	Without your parents? I bet that was one long party! *(Dan and Freddie laugh, Chris laughs uncomfortably)*
FREDDIE:	Well guys, we better get to class. Coming? *(Captain Coward gives the thumbs up sign; Captain Courage shakes his head sadly. The three guys head to class.)*

Scene 2
In class

(Chris, Dan, and Freddie are all sitting in a row, one in back of the other, with Chris in the middle seat. They're holding pens and taking a test. Mrs. Young is seated at the desk at the front of the class.)

DAN:	Psst...Chris! What is the answer to number two? *(Chris pretends he can't hear him)*
DAN:	*(kicks him lightly and whispers)* What's number two?
	(Captain Courage and Captain Coward pop out on either side of Chris. Chris assumes his blank look.)
CAPTAIN COWARD:	Come on, Chris, give him the answer!

CAPTAIN COURAGE: No, Chris, don't do it.

CAPTAIN COWARD: If you don't, he's gonna be mad, and he'll probably tell the other guys about it.

CAPTAIN COURAGE: Yeah, he might. But you'll feel good cause you took a stand.

FREDDIE: *(whispering to Chris)* Tell Dan the answer is B.

CHRIS: It's...uh...it's...I don't know.

FREDDIE: *(speaking up)* Dan, it's B!

MRS. YOUNG: Chris and Freddie, can I see you up front? *(Chris and Freddie walk up to her desk)*

MRS. YOUNG: What were you talking about?

FREDDIE: Oh, nothing, Mrs. Young. I was just telling Chris I hope he can get a B on his test.

MRS. YOUNG: Chris?

(Captain Courage and Captain Coward come racing to the front on either side of Chris, who assumes his blank look)

CAPTAIN COURAGE: Okay, Chris. This time you've got to be strong. You know what really happened. Tell the truth.

CAPTAIN COWARD: Oh yeah, that's great. You tell the truth and these guys will never speak to you again.

CAPTAIN COURAGE: Maybe not at first. But they'll respect you in the long run. If you go along with this lie, you'll feel terrible.

CAPTAIN COWARD: Maybe you'll feel a little bad at first. But the more you do it, the more you'll get used to it. And think of how popular you'll be! This is your chance to really get in with these guys.

CAPTAIN COURAGE: Don't do it, Chris!

CAPTAIN COWARD: Do it, Chris!

CAPTAIN COURAGE: No!

CAPTAIN COWARD: Yes!

page 3

SCRIPT 11.1

CHRIS:	*(puts both hands on his ears and shouts)* No!
MRS. YOUNG:	*(startled)* Okay, Chris. So what you're saying is that there was no cheating involved.
CHRIS:	I am? Oh yeah, I guess I am.
	(Captain Coward gives the champion sign again, and the two Captains exit)
MRS. YOUNG:	Thank you, boys. You may take your seats.
	(As Chris and Freddie take their seats, Dan high-fives Chris. The bell rings, and all three boys walk out of class.)
FREDDIE:	Hey, Chris, thanks a lot for covering for me. You were really cool.
DAN:	Yeah! Hey, by the way, Chris, what are you doing this weekend?
CHRIS:	*(feeling pretty bad)* Nothing.
DAN:	My parents are going to be out of town, and I'm having a party. Why don't you come?
FREDDIE:	Yeah, bud. It's going to be awesome. Monica is bringing some of her friends. And there'll be plenty of beer! *(Freddie and Dan both laugh)*
CHRIS:	I'll think about it.
DAN:	Okay, Chris. We'll see you tomorrow.
CHRIS:	See ya. *(Freddie and Dan exit, and Chris sits down and puts his face in his hands.)*

END

Daniel: No Fear

**Read aloud or skim the following Scriptures.
Use what you learn to discuss the related questions.**

Daniel chapter 1

1 Why didn't Daniel and his friends eat the royal food that the king offered them?

2 What was the result of their discipline? (v.15-17)

3 Have you ever had to discipline yourself for a sport, a diet or something else? How did it feel? What was the result?

Daniel 2:27-30

4 Because of his discipline, Daniel was given the ability to interpret dreams. When he interprets Nebuchadnezzar's dream, what does Daniel say to him about this ability?

5 Do you think this took courage? Why/Why not?

6 What does v.30 tell you about the kind of person Daniel was?

Daniel 2:46-48

7 What was Nebuchadnezzar's response after Daniel interpreted his dream?

8 What can we learn from Daniel (v.49) about the kind of friend he was? Do you have friends like that? Are you that kind of friend?

Daniel 3:1-4

9 How is Nebuchadnezzar's proclamation of faith in Daniel 2:47 different from Daniel's?

10 Is your faith more consistent (like Daniel's) or more wishy-washy (like Nebuchadnezzar's)?

Daniel 3:8-27

11 What do you learn about the courageous faith of Shadrach, Meshach, and Abednego?

12 Do you think Daniel's faith was strengthened by the company he kept?

13 Is your faith strengthened or weakened by the company you keep?

Daniel chapter 6

14 The new king, Darius, was so impressed by Daniel that he wanted to appoint him to administrate the whole kingdom. But the other leaders (out of their jealousy) convinced Darius to have everyone pray only to him, knowing this would trap Daniel. What was Daniel's response to this decree in Daniel 6:10?

15 Why do you think he was able to respond in this way? (Look especially at the last part of verse10.)

Daniel 6:16-23

16 Have you ever felt pressured to do something that, as a Christian, you didn't want to do? Were you able to respond the way Daniel did? Why or why not?

Daniel 6:25-27

17 What phrase does the king use in verses 16 and 20 to describe Daniel's faith?

18 What did this tell you about the condition of Daniel's faith?

19 How did Daniel's courage in his faith impact the rest of the kingdom?

20 What does this tell you about the influence our faith can have on others?

21 Have you ever shown your faith in such a way that others were influenced by it? If so, how? If not, why not?

COURAGE CHART
How'd you do today?

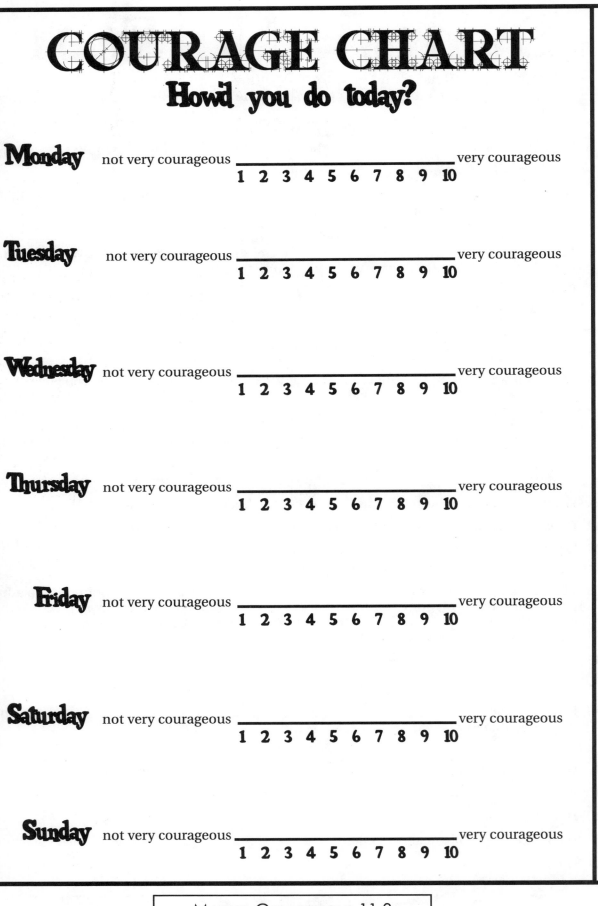

Monday not very courageous _____ very courageous
1 2 3 4 5 6 7 8 9 10

Tuesday not very courageous _____ very courageous
1 2 3 4 5 6 7 8 9 10

Wednesday not very courageous _____ very courageous
1 2 3 4 5 6 7 8 9 10

Thursday not very courageous _____ very courageous
1 2 3 4 5 6 7 8 9 10

Friday not very courageous _____ very courageous
1 2 3 4 5 6 7 8 9 10

Saturday not very courageous _____ very courageous
1 2 3 4 5 6 7 8 9 10

Sunday not very courageous _____ very courageous
1 2 3 4 5 6 7 8 9 10

SESSION TWELVE

JONAH
THE LONG WAY HOME

Jonah (the whole book!)

HERE'S THE POINT ▲

Sometimes we simply say no to God.

Sometimes, even though we know what God wants us to do, for some reason—peer pressure, fear, lack of incentive—we go the other way. But when we just say no to God, **we** are the losers. Jonah learned this lesson well.

Through Jonah's story we see how far we can go to try to get away from God. And more amazingly, we see how far God goes to bring us back.

▼ ▼ ▼ ▼ ▼ ▼ ▼ ▼ ▼

INTRO
Simon says

This oldie but goodie is an instant lesson in obedience.

You'll need...
• *no materials*

Have your students stand up, and tell them to do everything you say when you begin the instructions with the phrase "Simon says." (For example: "Simon says, stand on your right foot.") If you don't say "Simon says," no one should do what you say. Those who act on the instructions are out and must sit down. Move through your commands quickly, trying to trick students. (If you're no good at thinking on your feet, write out some of your commands.) Play as many rounds as it takes to get most of your students out.

Segue into your Bible lesson by saying—

The way to win this game was to do what Simon says. The way we win at life is to do what God says. Yet sometimes (for what ever reason), we don't do what God says—and usually we pay a price.

The story of Jonah shows us what can happen when we don't follow God's directions. As we talk about Jonah's experience, think about the times in your life when you've chosen not to follow God. From Jonah's life, learn that you're not automatically out of the game if you disobey; you just need to know to come back to God.

BIBLE LESSON

He ran, but he couldn't hide

Your talk covers the passages in Jonah that express his lesson of obedience. Here's a suggested outline:

JONAH'S CALL

Jonah 1:1-3

- Go over God's directions to Jonah and tell how Jonah responded.

- Talk about some of the reasons we don't do what God asks us to do.

- Give an illustration about a time you didn't do something you felt God was asking you to do—and what happened.

JONAH'S FIRST RESPONSE

Jonah 1:4-15

- Explain what happened to Jonah (and the people around him) when he didn't obey.

- Point out that the things that happened to Jonah were part of how God disciplined Jonah for not obeying him.

- Sometimes the bad things that happen in our lives are our own fault (though not always, as in the case of Job).

- God created the storm to guide Jonah back on track—a demonstration that God's discipline is motivated by love and grace, not petty revenge nor sheer meanness.

- As an additional gift of grace, the sailors came to recognize God as more powerful than their own gods.

- Sometimes God acts in spite of our disobedience.

JONAH'S FINAL RESPONSE

Jonah 1:17

- God provided a big fish to swallow Jonah to give Jonah some time to think and pray about his situation.

Jonah chapter 2

Contrast Jonah's response this time with his response at the beginning (1:3).

Prayer is our best response when God asks us to do something we don't want to do.

 Jonah chapter 3

Jonah ultimately obeyed God. As a result of listening to Jonah's proclamation, the Ninevites repented.

 Jonah chapter 4

Jonah's own heart had to be changed, too. He didn't think the Ninevites ought to get God's grace.

Through Jonah, God reminds us that he loves every person and desires all people to come to him.

GET UP & GET MOVING!

Jonah's jeopardized journey

You'll need...

- copies of **Jonah's Jeopardized Journey —Making Connections 12.1**
- pencils

Pass out this mixer to your students. Explain that they must complete each of the instructions with a different person or group of people. When they've finished an instruction, all the participants who worked together must initial the instruction. Have them all begin at the same time. The first two people to complete their worksheet— including having each instruction initialed—are the winners. As always, offering a prize increases the level of enthusiastic participation.

CUSTOM FIT

Use **My Journey** on a retreat. Send the kids outside to find a place where they can reflect quietly and individually and ask them to write out some of their own story.

Obeying God

You'll need...

- *copies of **Jonah: Obeying God— Small Group Q's 12.2***
- *copies of **My Journey—Making Connections 12.3***
- *pencils*
- *extra Bibles*

Hand out copies of both worksheets to your small groups. Following the discussion time, ask the kids to write out answers to the questions about their personal spiritual journeys. If you're short on time, send them home with **My Journey** for them to complete.

JONAH'S JEOPARDIZED JOURNEY

This mixer takes you through the journey of Jonah. You must complete every instruction. You can do them in any order—except the final instruction, which must be the last thing you do. Find different people for each leg of the journey, and get their signatures before you move on.

       The first two people to successfully complete the entire journey (with different signatures next to each instruction) are the winners.

Find 1 other person.
One of you will shout "Go!" while the
other shouts back "No!" Do this 5 times.
       Have the person sign here: _____

Find 3 other people.
Create a storm by first rubbing your
hands together. Then snap. Then pat your
legs. Then clap. Shout together, "Take Cover!"
       Have the people in your group sign here: _____

Find 2 other people.
Stand on your chairs and shout,
"Ahoy, Mate!" Give each other a sailor salute.
       Have them sign here: _____

Find 5 other people.
Lift up the smallest person in your group
and throw them at least two inches in the
air while you all say together, "You're going in!"
       Have someone in your group sign here: _____

Find 3 other people.
Choose one person to be Jonah. The
rest will join hands around Jonah and be
the big fish. Take 5 steps together, blowing
once after each step. The big fish counts to
three and burps together in Jonah's face.
       Have one of your group members sign here:_____

Find 1 other person.
       Have him or her sign your sheet first: _____
Measure between the two of you who is the
tallest. The tallest person is the tree and
carries the other person to the front of the
room shouting, "She's learned his lesson!"

The first pair to reach the front of the room wins.

JONAH
OBEYING GOD

Read aloud or skim the following Scriptures.
Use what you learn to discuss the related questions.

Jonah 1:1-3

1. What did Jonah do when God told him to go to Ninevah?

2. Can you relate to his response.

3. Have you ever done that to God?

Jonah 1:4

4. What did God do to Jonah?

5. Have you ever experienced God's storm in your life when you didn't obey him? If so, what was your storm like?

Jonah 1:5

6. What did Jonah do during the storm?

7. Have you ever tried to ignore God when he was speaking to you? What happened?

Jonah 1:7-16

8. How did God use the storm to bring the sailors to himself?

9. What does this tell you about the way God works—even when we're being disobedient?

Jonah 2

10. Have you ever felt what Jonah said he felt in his prayer?

11. What part of his prayer can you relate to the most? Why?

Jonah 3:1

12. What does this statement tell you about the way God works in our lives to get us to do what he wants us to do?

Jonah 2:4-5

13. Have you ever shared your faith with others? If so, what was their response?

Jonah 4:1-3

14. Have you ever been with someone who deserved to get punished and didn't? How did it make you feel?

15. Can you relate to Jonah's feelings in this passage?

Jonah 4:4-11

16. How did God teach Jonah a lesson in this chapter?

17. Has God ever used something to teach you a lesson? If so, what was it?

18. Is there anything he's been teaching you lately?

MY JOURNEY

Follow the map, answering the questions at each destination.
Reflect on your own journey with God.

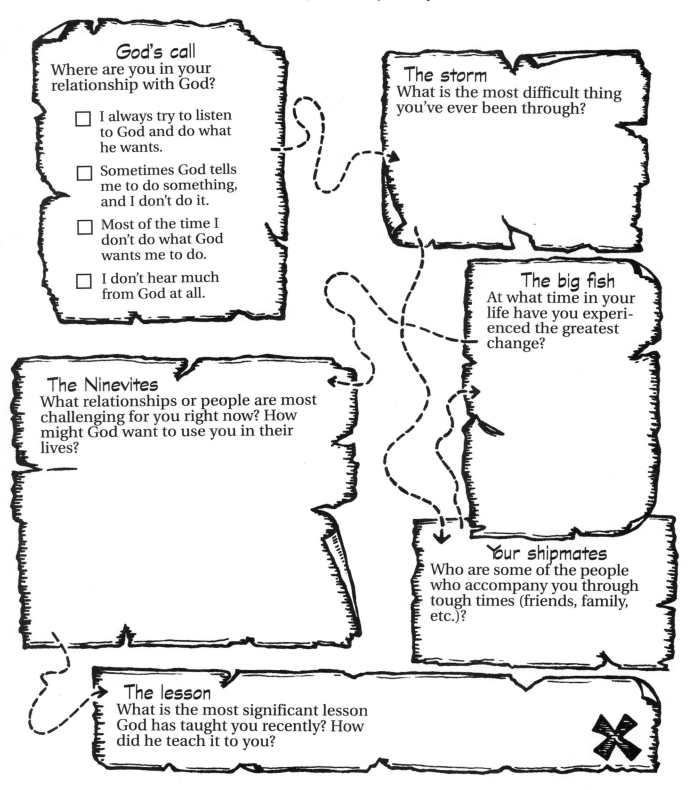

God's call
Where are you in your relationship with God?

☐ I always try to listen to God and do what he wants.

☐ Sometimes God tells me to do something, and I don't do it.

☐ Most of the time I don't do what God wants me to do.

☐ I don't hear much from God at all.

The storm
What is the most difficult thing you've ever been through?

The big fish
At what time in your life have you experienced the greatest change?

The Ninevites
What relationships or people are most challenging for you right now? How might God want to use you in their lives?

Your shipmates
Who are some of the people who accompany you through tough times (friends, family, etc.)?

The lesson
What is the most significant lesson God has taught you recently? How did he teach it to you?

Resources from Youth Specialties

Professional Resources

Administration, Publicity, & Fundraising (Ideas Library)
Developing Student Leaders
Equipped to Serve: Volunteer Youth Worker Training Course
Help! I'm a Junior High Youth Worker!
Help! I'm a Sunday School Teacher!
Help! I'm a Volunteer Youth Worker!
How to Expand Your Youth Ministry
How to Speak to Youth...and Keep Them Awake at the Same Time
Junior High Ministry (Updated & Expanded)
One Kid at a Time: Reaching Youth through Mentoring
A Youth Ministry Crash Course
The Youth Worker's Handbook to Family Ministry

Youth Ministry Programming

Camps, Retreats, Missions, & Service Ideas (Ideas Library)
Compassionate Kids: Practical Ways to Involve Your Students in Mission and Service
Creative Bible Lessons from the Old Testament
Creative Bible Lessons in John: Encounters with Jesus
Creative Bible Lessons in Romans: Faith on Fire!
Creative Bible Lessons on the Life of Christ
Creative Junior High Programs from A to Z, Vol. 1 (A-M)
Creative Meetings, Bible Lessons, & Worship Ideas (Ideas Library)
Crowd Breakers & Mixers (Ideas Library)
Drama, Skits, & Sketches (Ideas Library)
Dramatic Pauses
Facing Your Future: Graduating Youth Group with a Faith That Lasts
Games (Ideas Library)
Games 2 (Ideas Library)
Great Fundraising Ideas for Youth Groups
More Great Fundraising Ideas for Youth Groups
Great Retreats for Youth Groups
Greatest Skits on Earth
Greatest Skits on Earth, Vol. 2
Holiday Ideas (Ideas Library)
Hot Illustrations for Youth Talks
More Hot Illustrations for Youth Talks
Incredible Questionnaires for Youth Ministry
Junior High Game Nights
More Junior High Game Nights
Kickstarters: 101 Ingenious Intros to Just about Any Bible Lesson
Memory Makers
Play It! Great Games for Groups
Play It Again! More Great Games for Groups

Special Events (Ideas Library)
Spontaneous Melodramas
Super Sketches for Youth Ministry
Teaching the Bible Creatively
Up Close and Personal: How to Build Community in Your Youth Group
What Would Jesus Do? Youth Leader's Kit
Wild Truth Bible Lessons
Wild Truth Bible Lessons 2
Worship Services for Youth Groups

Discussion Starters

Discussion & Lesson Starters (Ideas Library)
Discussion & Lesson Starters 2 (Ideas Library)
4th-6th Grade TalkSheets
Get 'Em Talking
Keep 'Em Talking!
High School TalkSheets
More High School TalkSheets
High School TalkSheets: Psalms and Proverbs
Junior High TalkSheets
More Junior High TalkSheets
Junior High TalkSheets: Psalms and Proverbs
What If...? 450 Thought-Provoking Questions to Get Teenagers Talking, Laughing, and Thinking
Would You Rather...? 465 Provocative Questions to Get Teenagers Talking
Have You Ever...? 450 Intriguing Questions Guaranteed to Get Teenagers Talking

Clip Art

ArtSource Vol. 1—Fantastic Activities
ArtSource Vol. 2—Borders, Symbols, Holidays, and Attention Getters
ArtSource Vol. 3—Sports
ArtSource Vol. 4—Phrases and Verses
ArtSource Vol. 5—Amazing Oddities and Appalling Images
ArtSource Vol. 6—Spiritual Topics
ArtSource Vol. 7—Variety Pack
ArtSource Vol. 8—Stark Raving Clip Art
ArtSource CD-ROM (contains Vols. 1-7)

Videos

Edge TV
The Heart of Youth Ministry: A Morning with Mike Yaconelli
Next Time I Fall in Love Video Curriculum
Understanding Your Teenager Video Curriculum

Student Books

Grow For It Journal
Grow For It Journal through the Scriptures
What Would Jesus Do? Spiritual Challenge Journal
Wild Truth Journal for Junior Highers